Identification Solutions for Coordination Difficulties:

Dyspraxia,
Developmental Coordination Disorder (DCD)
and Handwriting

by Jan Poustie
B.Ed., (Dunelm), Cert Ed., Sharma Cert.,
R.S.A. Diploma SpLD, A.M.B.D.A

*This book, part of the Identification Solutions
for Specific Learning Difficulties Library,
is dedicated to my lovely daughters Briony and Alexandra
without whom it would never have been written.*

Contents

Appendix 5: © *Jan Poustie 2002.*

The checklists in this appendix may be photocopied by the owner of this book to enable a referral (or SpLD provision) for his/her students/children who have (or are believed to have) any of the conditions mentioned in this book. It is illegal to copy these pages for any other reason and anyone found doing so is liable to prosecution.

Foreword to the Identification Solutions for Specific Learning Difficulties Library

The Identification Solutions for Specific Learning Difficulties Library will be a valuable resource for parents, teachers and other professionals, as it clearly presents the indicators that can be observed in a range of specific learning difficulties and associated conditions.

Specialists in particular areas have been consulted and their advice, based on knowledge and experience, will certainly increase reader's understanding, making them more aware of the nature of the difficulties they are observing.

There is comprehensive information on where appropriate help, advice and diagnosis can be obtained. This, in itself, will relieve many anxieties – to take a book from a shelf and find a possible solution to problems will, hopefully, ensure that children and adults get the right help at the right time.

Violet Brand

This book was written to help both professionals and non-professionals find out the reasons why some individuals are failing to succeed and to provide information on where to turn to for help in overcoming their difficulties.

Books mentioned by number in this book (e.g. Book 1) refer to the books found in the Identification Solutions for Specific Learning Difficulties Library. Books found in this library are listed on the back cover of this book.

Identification Solutions for Coordination Difficulties by Jan Poustie   ISBN 1 901544 87 7

Help and Support

The following organisations provide conferences, information and telephone support.

Dyspraxia Foundation
8 West Alley, Hitchin, Herts, UK, SG5 1EG, Tel: 01462 454 986, Fax: 01462 455 052. Publishes 'Praxis II'. Website: www. dyspraxiafoundation.com
Email: dyspraxiafoundation@hotmail.com

Teen News
c/o Notts Dyspraxia Foundation, 21 Birchdale Avenue, Hucknall, Nottingham, NG15 6DL, Tel. 0115 9632220

Dyspraxia Foundation Adult Support Group
Contact: Mary Colley, 7 Sumatra Road, London, NW6 1PS
Tel: 020 7435 5443. Provides conferences, information and support.

Dyspraxia website for adults
www.dyspraxia-subscribe@yahoogroups.com

dyspraxia.nu
This organisation is run by teenagers for teenagers
www.dysf.fsnet.co.uk
E-mail: teenndf@hotmail.com
Helpline: 0115 963 2220.

The Dyspraxia Association
Contact: Aileen Tierney, 5 Blackglen Court, Sandyford, Dublin.

The Dyscovery Centre
12 Cathedral Road, Cardiff, CF1 9LJ
Tel: 01222 78866, Provides assessment and a remediation programme.

British Dyslexia Association
Helpline: Tel: 0118 966 8271, website: www.bda-dyslexia.org.uk/

Acknowledgements

Many grateful thanks go to the following educational and medical specialists:

<u>The first and second edition of this work</u>
Dr Ian McKinlay,
Senior lecturer in Community Child Health, Royal Manchester Children's Hospital.
Dr Rosemary Sassoon,
Specialist in the educational and medical aspects of handwriting and designer of the Sassoon family of typefaces for educational purposes.
Mary Nash-Wortham,
Speech therapist

<u>The first edition of this work on which the second edition is based</u>
Christine Stache,
Head Occupational Therapist, Musgrove Park Hospital, Taunton
Michèle Lee,
Chartered Physiotherapist in paediatrics
Dr Hamstra-Bletz,
Social scientist
Madeleine Portwood, Specialist Senior Educational Psychologist
Hugh Bellamy
Deputy Headteacher, West Somerset Community College.

The Dyspraxia Foundation
The Handwriting Interest Group
The Dyslexia Institute

Permissions
The copyright of the illustration of Callewaert's penhold on page 37 is owned by Dr Rosemary Sassoon. It has been reproduced in this book with the kind permission of Dr Rosemary Sassoon from her book *The Art and Science of Handwriting*, ISBN1871516331.

The views expressed by the author are her own and do not necessarily represent those who have contributed to, or assisted with the writing of this book.

Jan Poustie

Word from the author

I've cracked it, I actually did it! Today, in late autumn 2001, I drove through the beautiful gold and scarlet-leaved country lanes of Somerset in 5th gear!!!! Not so wonderful I hear you say but I am one of the minority of the population who has Dyspraxia and who can also drive. Thirty years ago I managed to master driving with four gears but like many of those with Dyspraxia I find it very difficult to modify a movement-based skill once I have learned it. It has taken me twenty years to pluck-up the courage to finally achieve my goal of conquering 5th gear without killing myself or my passengers.

There seems to have been little or no research conducted into the inheritance factor of Dyspraxia/DCD but it is obvious to those of us who work in the field that there must be one. So often we see similar difficulties (or other SpLD Profile conditions) in parents and their children. Both my children have Dyspraxia; but finding that out was not easy – there are so many sub-groups of Dyspraxia/DCD and each of them is assessed by a different professional. What many people do not realise is that we usually have academic-based problems too – often literacy, numeracy, language and social skills development are affected too.

Teasing (gentle or otherwise) is the bane of our lives. It is so easy to gently ridicule us for what we cannot do. It is so difficult for us to have high self-esteem because we are constantly being reminded of our inadequacies. Dyspraxia is not just about problems with the planning and organisation of movement, it's the way that these movement-based skills affect so much of our lives. Incidents happen on a daily basis for those of us who are clumsy. The broken china, the bruised leg, the knocked over glass of milk – our difficulties affect not only ourselves but those around us.

But not all of those who have Dyspraxia/DCD are clumsy. If only certain areas of motor functioning are affected such as the movements of the eyes (e.g. Occulomotor Dyspraxia) then the individual may move with grace and may even have highly developed spatial skills (unlike many of us with Dyspraxia/DCD). A great difficulty for many of us is the achieving of well-presented handwritten work. Handwriting still dominates the thinking of many educators. Far too many only think in terms of making the child produce a good well-formed script. Unfortunately, with our worksheet-dominated special needs education system this

Travelling has been the bane of my life. From severe travel sickness (often an accompaniment to Dyspraxia) which caused me to have to walk everywhere to struggling with the gears on both cars and bikes. Not that I've been using my bike much recently, ever since one of the pedals fell off whilst I was riding it - it is incredibly difficult to ride a one-pedalled bike! I could not cope with the gear controls when they were not located on the handlebars. I just could not trust that I would be able to balance, reach down and move the gear whilst still keeping the handlebars under control.

usually results in the student (especially at primary school) wading through handwriting worksheet after worksheet. Too few teachers know of the many practical activities that can be used to help improve writing skills (and which are much more fun to do, see page 30 for details).

Far too many teachers doggedly make the child carry on with doing handwriting worksheets even when it has become obvious that they are no longer achieving an improvement in handwriting. Far too few of our students have good access to computers and so cannot show their knowledge base simply because even if they can write neatly they can only do it at an exceptionally slow speed. This aspect of education is so important that I have discussed it in great detail in the conclusion of this book.

I was a new mum, pretty exhausted from a baby who only slept for six hours out of every twenty-four. No-one noticed her problems so I just ploughed on with life. No problems with learning to walk (she achieved this by ten months). Since she didn't sleep she went to the park at least once a day (often at night in the summer). It was one of the best things that we could have done to help develop her co-ordination skills – we did it not to improve her skills but because we were desperately trying to tire her out so that she would go to sleep

It was the language that I knowingly noticed first and problems with doing jigsaws. The health visitor was not concerned, she passed her developmental milestones assessment test (but of course being awake for eighteen hours a day meant that she had a lot more experience of movement than most children her age). All children are different I said to myself and I ploughed on with life again. She started to read before she went to school. She had been ready to learn to read since she was two and a half years old; in fact she had known which way up print was since the age of ten months! However, I delayed teaching her to read fearing that it would make it difficult for both her and her teacher if she was too far in advance of her peers. She knew her letter sounds but odd – she couldn't build or break down words with them. Her fantastic visual memory more than made up for that problem! I ignored the phonics and taught her to read visually; her reading developed at an astonishing fast rate, she could read at 150 word per minute by the age of five years. But, her first year of school was a struggle, she was repeatedly told off for not keeping within the lines when colouring – writing was definitely not going so smoothly.

Unfortunately, both medical and educational professionals may not notice the early signs of motor co-ordination difficulties. Thus none of the medical professionals with whom my children came into contact recognised the signs of Dyspraxia. The midwife, paediatric nurse, health visitor and GP; none of them realised that having to breast feed a baby thirteen times a day (oh I remember, it well!), who then went on to eat very, very slowly, could not pronounce her own name and who found it exceptionally difficult to swallow tablets was definitely a candidate for Verbal (Articulatory) Dyspraxia.

She had never had any problems in making friends at playgroup and nursery but now was struggling to do so.

By the time my elder daughter was seven years old I had become pretty worried, I'm remembering and noticing all sorts of things. All sorts of words were (and are being) mispronounced by my daughter, or she was placing the emphasis on the wrong part of the word. She was fussy about the texture of foods and fabrics. Her movements just did not look tidy. Despite plenty of practice in the local park she struggled to hold her weight on the monkey bars. Why was it such a huge struggle for her to learn to ride a bike and to roller blade? She desperately wanted to learn the violin but oh the huge problems we had with learning that. Something was definitely odd here but what was it? Like many parents of children who have Dyspraxia/DCD I had lots of questions - but no answers.

Then we noticed the maths! By the age of seven years it was only too apparent that she was struggling with both the language and concepts of maths. Her teacher saw no problems and so that led me to learn all about Dyscalculia (a specific learning difficulty in mathematics) and eventually led to me lecturing and writing books on the subject.

Then, looking for solutions for my younger daughter's reading problems, I attended a local British Dyslexia Association taster course for teachers where I was able to borrow books from the tutors. I find a gem - a single paragraph in a book about Dyslexia that describes Dyspraxia. It is almost impossible to describe in words how I felt. It was like being given the key to a fortune in jewels I suddenly knew what was wrong, I still did not know about the sub-groups but I knew what the main condition was. My daughter (now aged ten years) stared out at me from the pages of that book - and so I realised did I. If she had Dyspraxia then so did I.

As I researched into my daughter's problems all my struggles to achieve qualifications, master co-ordination skills started to fall into place. At last I understood why I had had such a struggle and I was determined that my children would not travel the same path. Now I had a name for it, I was able to access its national charity (the Dyspraxia Foundation) and work out who I had to make a referral to in order to obtain a diagnosis. After seeing the consultant paediatrician he was able to refer her to a paediatric

My younger daughter was very different. The speed of her language development was astonishing but, she did have problems with doing jigsaws. That was odd as I could see that she had no problems with handling tools and her pouring of liquids skills were superb.

Of course in the end I found out that she had Occulomotor Dyspraxia (which affects the movements of the eyes). So yes she could handle tools but she couldn't clearly see the picture on the jigsaw pieces! She also couldn't see text properly which led to major problems in learning to read (see Book 4). Now a teenager, I delight in watching her enjoy reading complex texts. As she says,
"I am slow, but I can read!"

Identification Solutions for Coordination Difficulties by Jan Poustie   ISBN 1 901544 87 7

Many individuals will need help to adopt strategies that will enable them to overcome many of the difficulties caused by Dyspraxia/DCD. Some will find that the difficulties become apparent again when under stress and/or illness.

occupational therapist (POT) who amazingly had an unbelievably short waiting list (it can often take two or more years to see a POT nowadays).

That of course was only the beginning. Like many others who find the SpLD Profile conditions present within their family members we have had to commit much of our family's resources of time, energy and money to overcoming the difficulties these conditions cause. Throughout her life we have had to teach our elder daughter the social skills that other students just pick up naturally. We have had to give her help with developing her motor co-ordination and speech and language skills plus a huge amount of help with mathematics. Now, few people who meet her realise the hurdles she has conquered through our support and her determination. They see an exceptionally intelligent young lady who has mastered many skills. They see someone who has gained good passes at GCSE and is now taking A levels at a 6th form college where, in the space of just a few months she has made many friends and her level of work is already starting to exceed the initial grade predictions made when she entered college. We have succeeded.

I did not wake up one day and decide to become a specialist in specific learning difficulties and certainly in my wildest dreams I would not have thought of lecturing or writing books. Yes, I was a teacher who specialised in special educational needs but in fact (like the majority of the teachers that I knew) I had virtually no knowledge of specific learning difficulties at all. My children changed all that. It was because none of the educational and medical professionals with whom my children came into contact could recognise their difficulties that I had to find out the sources of my children's problems. My search to find strategies to overcome their problems led me to conducting the intensive research that has made this library possible.

My children were lucky, many others (and their parents and the professionals who work with them) are not so lucky. Reliable identification can change the lives of all of those involved with the student and this library has been designed so that that change can occur. I hope that the information in this book enables your lives to change as much as it did mine.

Jan

CHAPTER 1
The Identification of Developmental Dyspraxia /DCD

PART 1 – Understanding

Development Coordination Disorder /Dyspraxia – what do we call it?
During the last few years, there has been a change in terminology and various professionals are coming up with different terms and subgroups. This is making the whole world of Dyspraxia a little confusing both for professionals and non-professionals alike. The term Developmental Coordination Disorder (DCD) is used by some as an umbrella term for all motor-based learning difficulties (when such difficulties are present from birth). The medical sector prefer to use this term and the diagnostic criteria for it are stated in the worldwide recognised DSM IV and ICD 10. Some medical professionals believe that Developmental Dyspraxia is a sub-group of DCD but others see it as a separate condition. Some professionals (e.g. occupational therapists) use the term Developmental Dyspraxia when perceptual difficulties are seen alongside the coordination difficulties. The educational and the charitable sectors (and many parents) appear to favour the term Developmental Dyspraxia (DD). Somewhere in amongst all this is another term (Sensory Integration Disorder) which some feel is part of DCD while others believe it to be a separate condition or DCD sub-group; others believe it is simply Developmental Dyspraxia by another name. Just to make things more confusing, some medical professionals use the term Dyspraxia for any problem that results in coordination difficulties. (See *Dyspraxia: The Hidden Handicap* by Dr A Kirby for further details of these definitions.) Now that this is all 'as clear as mud' the reader will realise that for the lay person (and the professional) the area of DCD/DD has become something of a minefield.

The author has chosen to use both the abbreviations DCD/DD and the term Developmental Dyspraxia in this book. She has chosen to adopt Madeleine Portwood's definition of the latter; i.e.

> Developmental Dyspraxia is the result of neurological immaturity which affects the function of the right hemisphere and consequently the individual shows evidence of auditory and/or visual perceptual difficulties, motor planning and organisation.

Developmental Dyspraxia has been defined as a Specific Learning Difficulty in gross- and fine-motor planning which is not

Case study: Alice
DCD/DD is often accompanied by emotional fragility which is often not understood by professionals. Thus the student can be emotionally devastated by incidents that other students will take in their stride. This very bright girl had been playing in school concerts for ten years, her parents had attended all of them. When she was in Year 11 she took part in a concert. Her parents arrived late and just missed her playing her piece. The girl was not on stage again for over an hour. She spent much of that hour sobbing in the girl's toilets. Both teachers and parents can find such behaviours so 'over the top' that they cannot support the child when s/he becomes emotionally devastated.

Dressing difficulties can make trying on clothes in shops, getting ready for school in the morning and changing for PE, swimming and drama particularly stressful.

Causes of Developmental Dyspraxia
In many cases there appears to be a link between the presence of Developmental Dyspraxia and difficulties during pregnancy, labour and birth. (See *Developmental Dyspraxia* by M. Portwood). Diet is another factor; with a significant group having metabolic dysfunctioning (see Portwood's book and Book 1 of this library). There also appears to be a genetic factor as one often sees more than one member of the direct (and extended) family group having the condition and/or one of the other Specific Learning Difficulties Profile conditions.

caused by muscle/nerve damage. It is believed to affect between 5–10 percent of the population with:

> approximately 10,000 children being affected in the UK. It affects both sexes, with three affected boys for every two affected girls. However, the ratio known to the professional services is four boys to one girl. This is because boys are more likely to respond by behaving badly. Girls are more likely to be anxious or depressed but less conspicuous. [1]

An individual who has DCD/DD may have both fine and gross motor control difficulties, or, only one of them. Gross motor control is related to whole limb/body movements. Fine motor control is related to hand/finger movements, the organs of speech and eye movements. Each individual will have a unique array of difficulties, which are likely to affect many aspects of his/her life. Most people appear to believe that clumsiness is always part of DCD/DD but this is not the case.

The need for training and professional specialist status
More worrying than the controversy over the correct term to use is the fact that people with comparatively little knowledge are latching on to the DCD/DD bandwagon and offering assessment, support and advice without the necessary knowledge base. AMBDA (Associate Member of the British Dyslexia Association) status is awarded by the BDA to (mainly) educational professionals who have the necessary experience, training and knowledge base to assess intellectual ability, diagnose Dyslexia and provide a teaching programme for it. It is of concern to many of us that we do not as yet have a specialist status for professionals who specialise in DCD/DD similar to that of AMBDA. In order for such a status to exist we will have to accept that some professionals with an educational background are able to diagnose Developmental Dyspraxia. Needless to say, there are many in the medical sector who would not be happy with this, as it involves the risk of conditions other than DCD/DD being missed. However, the chronic shortage of paediatric physio/occupational therapists means that for the individual to have any opportunity of receiving a diagnosis and support we may have little choice but to go along this route. In order to do so, the Dyspraxia Foundation would need to have the facilities to determine who gains the equivalent of AMBDA status in Dyspraxia; e.g. Associate Membership of the Dyspraxia Foundation (AMDF).

There are many practitioners who are already known to be highly skilled in this area (both in the medical and educational sectors) who could be awarded such status (e.g. AMDFE for educationalists and AMDFM for medical professionals). Defining AMDFE would be relatively simple if we copied the criteria used for the AMBDA award, which include the awardee being able to conduct assessments of intellectual functioning. This could be achieved by adding a DCD/DD module to the present highly regarded OCR Diploma in Specific Learning Difficulties. However, that still leaves us with the problem that the Dyspraxia Foundation would need to find the time, personnel and finances to oversee such a scheme.

The different types of Developmental Dyspraxia

As there are many types of Developmental Dyspraxia, no one person will show all of the various indicators. Generally speaking, the easiest individuals to recognise will be those having the common indicators (see Table 1, pages 14-16). The most difficult individuals to recognise are those who have only one key indicator from Table 1. Such individuals may also have one sensory perception indicator from Table 2. They may have several, or all, of the other indicators relevant to a particular subgroup of Dyspraxia; for example:

▸ Verbal (Articulatory) Dyspraxia: see page 4 and side panel.

▸ Oral Dyspraxia: see side panel this page.

▸ Occulomotor Dyspraxia: see Book 4.

▸ Ideomotor Dyspraxia: difficulties in doing single motor tasks, such as picking up a cup.

▸ Ideational Dyspraxia: difficulties in planning and carrying out a sequence of operations. For example, though able to pick up shoe polish, duster and shoes, the individual cannot carry out the task of polishing the shoes.

▸ Constructional Dyspraxia: difficulties in creating a duplicate of a model due to an inability to know how to place things in relation to one another; for example Lego™.

▸ Dressing Dyspraxia: this has two forms. Fifty per cent of children who have Dyspraxia have gross-motor problems. Most of this group are likely to have problems with dressing and undressing at some stage. [2] Dressing difficulties can make trying on clothes in shops, getting ready for school in the morning and changing for PE, swimming and drama particularly stressful. Students can struggle to remember the order in which to put the clothes on (and how to arrange their body and the clothes) in order to get dressed. As a result, clothes can end up inside out and back to front. [3] There is a much less common form, which causes the individual to only dress and groom one side of the body.

A disadvantage of going along the route of educational professionals making a diagnosis of DCD/DD is that medical professionals are more likely to be aware of conditions (other than DCD/DD) that can be characterised by motor co-ordination difficulties.

Definitions of terms

'Verbal Dyspraxia
This is used as an umbrella term to include all aspects of speech and language where there is:
an expressive language dysfunctioning (relating to the thought processes which are neurologically controlled in the brain). It is seen as problem in recording information* and in speaking information; e.g. sentence construction and so on.
as well as an oral difficulty relating specifically to movement of the musculature to move the lips, tongue and soft palate (the latter is in the roof of the mouth).

Oral Dyspraxia
This is used when only an oral difficulty is present.'
(Mary Nash-Wortham, MRCSLT)

Note: * refers to getting one's thoughts down on paper not the actual handwriting.

Identification Solutions for Coordination Difficulties by Jan Poustie   ISBN 1 901544 87 7

Textural sensitivity (liking/disliking soft/rough textures to touch or in the mouth) is another indicator of DCD/DD that is easily spotted in the early years.

The Nuffield Hearing and Speech Centre Dyspraxia Programme
This provides ideas and materials for speech and language therapists to use in their management of children with Verbal (Articulatory) Dyspraxia. Its materials cover most of the oro-motor, sound production and sound-sequencing activities that children who have Dyspraxia will need to practice. For further information contact:
Tel. 020 7915 1535.

Oral and Verbal (Articulatory) Dyspraxia

Difficulties can be seen in various aspects of speech; for example, correct breathing for speech; keeping speech understandable in long sentences; controlling the speed, rhythm and volume of speech; saying particular sounds, such as 'th' and 'thr'; pronouncing parts of words in the correct order and the swallow reflex. (Also see Book 4.)

Case Study: Harry

Early identification results in the student having a better chance of achieving success even if his/her form of Dyspraxia is quite severe. Harry was three and a half years old when he was diagnosed as having Verbal (Articulatory) Dyspraxia.

By about eighteen months, Harry's parents were aware that there was a speech problem but decided not to involve professionals at that time. When he was three years old they realised that other children were speaking fluently whilst he was not. He spoke a lot but those around him found it was impossible to understand what he was saying, which resulted in him being very frustrated. The health visitor gave Harry a hearing test and found no problem but realised that there was definitely a problem with speech.

He was referred to a speech therapist (a six month wait for the assessment) who advised the parents that his difficulties would take a long time to resolve. He received speech therapist intervention in six-weekly blocks for several years. Just before starting school, his parents and the speech therapist were becoming increasingly concerned about his fine-motor skills so he was referred to a paediatrician. She confirmed that motor coordination difficulties were present and referred Harry to a paediatric occupational therapist (OT). It was felt by all the professionals (including the OT) that Harry would be able to cope with mainstream school.

For the next two years, Harry attended mainstream school, with speech therapy being provided after school once a week. (Throughout all this time, the parents were involved in supporting their son's skill acquisition by doing daily exercises; for example, tongue and lip exercises, under the supervision of the speech therapist.) Meanwhile, school was aware that Harry's problems were hindering his learning of reading and writing. He had a good general knowledge but his written work did not reflect this. In Year 2 he was referred for a Statement of Special Education Needs and put on to the waiting list for the Speech and Language Unit, which he entered when he was seven years old.

Harry's parents were aware that he was already very self-conscious about his problems and they were quite worried that transferring him to a special unit (where he would be educated away from the other children in his neighbourhood) would make this worse. Interestingly enough he did manage to maintain his friendships with those in his neighbourhood (through attendance at Cubs, parents inviting them home for tea and so on). However, once he returned to mainstream school he found that the friends had formed new groups of friends within school and in that setting they did not know how to include him.

He was supplied with daily LEA transport during his time at the special unit as this was some way away from home. He stayed there for three years and then moved back into mainstream primary for one year, where in the final term he was supplied with a laptop computer. Transfer back to his primary school was not easy because the primary school believed that they could not meet his needs even though they were given plenty of Learning Support Assistant (LSA) hours funded by the LEA. Part of the problem was that the mainstream school had very low expectations of Harry and he resented the fact that he was put into the remedial maths group. Even though he was better at maths than the rest of the group the school refused to move him up. (Four years on, this is still a strong memory for Harry.) He surprised the school by achieving a Level 4 in maths and science in the Keystage 2 SATs.

His last annual review at primary school was attended by the assistant SENCO from his future secondary school and this enabled the school to ensure that his transfer to secondary school went smoothly. His Statement continued for the next three years. (As well as regular special needs support for spelling and reading he was also taught to touch type and within the first two years he was able to type at well over forty words per minute.) By the end of Year 9, Harry had made so much progress that the LEA withdrew the Statement (which the parents were happy to accept). Interestingly enough, although language problems commonly accompany Dyspraxia, Harry was never found to have any. At the end of Keystage 2, Harry was only able to achieve Level 3 in English. Much to his parent's delight, Harry achieved Level 6 in both English and Maths in the Keystage 3 SATs, which just shows what can be achieved with the right provision.

Other students who have Oral or Verbal Dyspraxia may not require attendance at a specialist unit in order to improve their skills as the following case study shows.

Modify PE activities so that the child with DCD/DD is enabled to participate

His mum stuck some candles on a piece of board and Harry was encouraged to create the 'p' sound by blowing out a candle whilst he said words such as 'pop', 'poppy' and so on.

Frederick's uneven intellectual profile is common when DCD/DD is present, though some students may show an even profile. The Ravens is usually used by teachers. The WISC and the BAS are used by educational psychologists but it is important to note that they are not identical; their sub-tests do not assess for exactly the same things; e.g. the BAS arithmetic sub-test assesses maths whereas the WISC III UK arithmetic assesses both maths and mathematical language. Portwood (in her book *Developmental Dyspraxia*) writing about the WISC III UK states that:

> 'Some tests appear to present particular difficulties in more than 90% of dyspraxic youngsters: they are arithmetic, coding and block design.'

Each SpLD Profile condition can be reflected in the sub-test results; e.g. if Similarities is weak then look for a language problem, see Book 3. Each sub-group of Dyspraxia will affect different sub-test results; e.g. if the WISC Picture Completion and Block Design scores are low then look for Occulomotor Dyspraxia, see Book 4. Some students can have visual-spatial and visual-perceptual scores in the superior range but still have a form of Occulomotor Dyspraxia (see case study Bethany in Book 4).

Case Study: Frederick (13 years)

Frederick was struggling to read his own writing, and had a spelling age three years below his reading age. Initial assessment (using the Ravens Progressive Matrices) revealed an IQ of 125+. A later assessment (using the WISC III UK) showed that he had a very uneven intellectual profile with his Performance IQ being much lower than his Verbal IQ. He had difficulties in saying sounds; e.g. 'thr' and 'th'. He also 'mumbled' the middle sounds of long words and was unsure as to what the sounds should be. (As pronunciation affects spelling, this problem had to be corrected.)

A variety of apparatus, and his love of the violin, were used to help his spelling skills. Frederick used different patterns of bowing on the violin to represent the syllables. He used it to represent the long and short sounds too whilst he said the sound patterns; for example, 'the throbbing thrush threw the thread'. The *Tok Back* device (which is worn around the head to enable the student to hear his/her own voice better) was used in combination with the mirror from the *Edith Norrie Letter Case* . This enabled him to simultaneously hear and see what he said whilst watching the lips of the author. The letters in the *Eddie Norrie Letter Case* are especially useful for those who have speech difficulties. The recording facility of the *Wordshark 2* computer program was also used to help his pronunciation difficulties and to teach him to spell and read. A *Franklin* spellchecker boosted his self-esteem as through its use he was able to beat his Gran at Scrabble – something he had been trying to do for several years! *Readers who want to find more about Frederick's provision should go to Chapter 2.*

Various difficulties are seen alongside Dyspraxia

➤   Writing difficulties (handwriting difficulties may also be present due to Graphomotor Dyspraxia) *(see Chapter 2)*

➤   Both numeracy *(see Mathematics Solutions: an introduction to Dyscalculia,* pub. Next Generation*)* and speech/language difficulties *(see Book 4)* are usually associated with it. [4]

➤   Behavioural difficulties and social difficulties (e.g. the way in which the pupil interacts with his/her peers).

Early recognition is vital when DCD/DD is present if the child is to reach his/her potential

As so many areas are affected, it is often necessary to obtain a full picture of the individual's strengths and weaknesses. This is achieved via a multidisciplinary assessment, which involves several different specialists assessing for different conditions. Severe DCD/DD is very apparent even to the lay person, and it is likely to be recognised at the preschool stage by professionals such as Health Visitors and doctors during routine developmental checks. This is especially the case if the child's main difficulties are in motor control (body, limb, hand or speech movements rather than behaviour, vision etc.). However, in some cases, the individual has a low-level of several conditions. When the difficulties caused by each condition are added together they can markedly affect the individual's life and create a considerable problem in learning. It is this 'moderate specific' group which is likely to be found in non-specialist schools and which may be missed by both educational and medical professionals. Recognition of such children may often only be made if professionals ask the parents about the presence of various indicators of Dyspraxia (as mentioned in Tables 1 and 2, pages 14-16) and then talk to their colleagues in the relevant professions. Table 3, pages 17-18 (which mainly relates to gross-motor functioning) and Table 4, pages 19-22 (which mainly relates to fine-motor functioning) provide more detailed information on specific areas of functioning that may be affected. These tables use the terms that medical professionals use when assessments are made.

Delayed development or DCD/DD?

The associated features of Developmental Dyspraxia (see Table 1) and what appear to be difficulties in motor planning/organisation can be seen in both late developers and in those with Dyspraxia. At the playgroup/nursery stage, it can be very apparent that a child lacks rhythm and/or appears less coordinated than his/her peers. The latter can be because the child is not given enough opportunities at home to develop coordination skills. Many of our children have too little experience of physical movement. (They no longer walk to school and they focus on play activities that are sedentary in nature, such as sitting in front of a computer screen and handheld computer games.) This lack of physical activity is even affecting our babies, who may be secured in a carrier and not removed from it when visiting granny (for example) and who may not be allowed to play on the floor because of society's obsession with hygiene. To avoid unnecessary referrals, unless the DCD/DD is severe (e.g. very noticeable compared with his/her peer group), the first course of action is to provide concentrated practice and exposure to a variety of physical activities. [5] Otherwise, the physio/occupational therapists may find that most causes for concern have disappeared when they eventually see the child many months later.

Associated features that can be spotted early

A dislike of having ones hair/nails touched and/or cut is commonly associated with Dyspraxia. This needs to be brought

Contacts for teaching materials

Tok Back
Taskmaster: Tel: 0116 2704286

Wordshark 3
Tel: 020 8748 5927
This is the latest version of this program.

Edith Norrie Letter Case
Tel: 01945 463441

Shoulder girdle weakness
Students who have this weakness can find PE particularly difficult when activities involve the shoulders as the controlling force (e.g. netball) and/or have to take the body weight (e.g. climbing ropes, press ups). This difficulty is also likely to cause pain (which is often considerable) for the older child/adult when:

▸▸ hanging out washing at above shoulder height,

▸▸ painting ceilings and the walls that are above shoulder height,

▸▸ spring-cleaning top shelves

▸▸ writing at the top of a white/ blackboard.

Also see page 20.

to the attention of all those who work with young children. All of us who are parents or who work with young children know that many children dislike having their hair washed, but when Developmental Dyspraxia is present the reaction of the child to this process often has to be seen to be believed. This dislike carries on for many years, even into the teenage years and adulthood. Textural sensitivity (liking/disliking soft/rough textures to touch or in the mouth) is another indicator that is easily spotted in the early years.

The 'it's not Dyslexia' individual

Sometimes, children who have either low-level or moderate DCD/DD pass through all the usual early health checks without their condition being recognised. Since many teachers are unaware of the indicators of DCD/DD, these children can go through the whole educational system without being picked up, 'though there may be emotional/behavioural problems, including signs of anxiety, depression or withdrawal, including school refusal or poor attendance attributed to frequent minor illness'. [6] The parents of such children may become concerned and ask for an assessment of Dyslexia to be made. The teacher makes a preliminary assessment of the child (e.g. spelling and reading) but finds little or no areas of concern in literacy. (There may well be a noticeable problem with presentation of work and handwriting, but this may be put down to carelessness and/or laziness.) Consequently, the teacher informs the parent that the child is 'not dyslexic' but s/he does not refer the child for DCD/DD because s/he does not know the relevant indicators. The child may then struggle throughout his/her academic life and, in the worst scenario, may have both teachers and parents nagging him/her because she is not trying hard enough. S/he may even written off as being 'not that bright'.

Transfer from primary to secondary school

When DCD/DD is present we are likely to see poor planning and organisation skills. Time-keeping skills may also be poor. Individuals may find it difficult to relate to their peer group or the rules of lots of different teachers; the latter can be a problem in the secondary environment. Although the poor time-keeping skills may cause a great deal of difficulty for some children many are just able to cope with the primary-school situation. However, the demands on these skills at secondary-school level plus the inconsistent approach of the different subject teachers may overwhelm them. Even bright children may need considerable support from the Learning Support

Individuals are likely to need to be taught the presentation skills that are needed in most lessons; e.g. drawing charts, underlining using a ruler and presenting maths work neatly. Such provision will reduce the stress felt by the pupil and enable him/her to have the opportunity to reach his/her potential in adulthood.

Department and may become school refusers if they are not handled carefully. They can become more aware of their weaknesses in the secondary-school environment as set segments of the day are devoted to different subjects. Thus, they may find it very stressful when a day has nothing but motor-planning-based subjects, such as CDT, Art, PE and Cooking.

If stress-induced illness (or frequent withdrawal from class for teaching/therapy) causes students to miss lessons, then more stress is created as they try to catch up on work. This can result in them being under so much stress that they can no longer face attending school at the end of the week. In such cases, the stress can be reduced by allowing them to attend for some 'short days' (for example, the first two lessons of the day only). Also either allow them to attend the learning support department for a particularly stressful lesson, or provide learning support within the lesson. It is very important that parents and school work together in such situations to help the child overcome his/her difficulties. It is also important that all those involved with the pupil realise that it may take weeks/ months rather than days of such provision before the pupil has settled into a new environment.

Many of the subjects at secondary level involve the use of mathematical skills. The student will also have a maths lesson nearly every school day. As a result, students who have both DCD/DD and Dyscalculia may have no days in the week when they are not under stress.

Transfer from secondary school to further education
At times of transfer, preparation is the key. Various strategies can be used to make transfer easier.

➤ Make sure that the student has plenty of opportunities to visit the college and meet the Learning Support Department staff and visit the department before attending the college. (Note: each college will have its own name for this department.)

➤ If opportunities arise for a 'taster' course then take it. Sometimes, these are held during the summer holiday whilst the student is in Year 10. Again, make sure that you have discussed the student's needs with the organiser of the course beforehand.

➤ Even if the student has become used to travelling to school by him/herself it might be wise to drive the student to college for the first few days, as stress may affect already weak road-safety skills. This will also mean that there is less of a rush to get out of the house. (The parent can always drop the student off round the corner from the college so that there is no problem with being teased by the peer group because the student is being taken to college.)

➤ If possible, make sure that a parent is available (on the end

It seems that the 'clumsiness' of youth is not regarded as a major problem in adulthood when Dyspraxia is present

of a phone) so that if things do get a bit sticky then the student/college will have a number to ring.

▸▸ Prior to starting at the college, verbally rehearse with the student his/her first day so that s/he works out where s/he will go at break and at lunch time, the route s/he will take to each lecture, and the teachers s/he will have for each lecture.

▸▸ Ask the student what areas s/he has worries about in going to college so that you can discuss with him/her the different situations that s/he might find him/herself in.

▸▸ Reduce the workload so that the student is under less stress. So, if the student is very capable (and students of his/her ability would normally be taking four or five A/S Levels) then reduce it to three or four. This advice applies to all of our SpLD students. Note: if the student is likely to want to go on to Higher Education (HE) for example, university, then look ahead to what s/he wants to do as a career. Make sure that the A/S Level courses are of the right type (and will have enough points) to enable him/her to go on to appropriate HE courses.

Adult Developmental Dyspraxia

Professionals view the continuation of Developmental Dyspraxia into adulthood in different ways. In the past, it was more common to believe that few individuals experience problems as an adult, though some believed that it usually continued into adulthood. Research in this area is limited with some evidence showing that Developmental Dyspraxia does continue into adulthood for a larger group (Losse et al's ten year follow-up study of individuals aged five to fifteen years showed no evidence of growing out of Dyspraxia[7]). The latter may not be obvious because individuals use coping strategies in both their choice of job and leisure pursuits to avoid problems associated with their Dyspraxia.[8] It is thought that such adults are likely to be of above average intelligence and to possess resilience and determination. [9] It also seems that the 'clumsiness' of youth is not regarded as a major problem by adults. Instead, it is often the difficulties found alongside Dyspraxia that become the dominant difficulties in adulthood (see examples in side panel).

Daily living and DCD/DD

Movement of some sort is needed for most of our daily tasks. Such tasks range from personal hygiene, eating, moving around the school/workplace and maintaining an appropriate posture throughout the day. For the adult, the 'final straw' may be the preparation of a meal at the end of the day. Once adults become parents they then have to use their inadequate skills to cope with more demanding tasks relating to childcare. Changing the baby and doing up nappies so

Difficulties found alongside Developmental Dyspraxia in adulthood

▸▸ difficulties in overflow movements (such as moving the arms when it is only necessary to move the legs), dancing, keeping fit,

▸▸ a lack of rhythm, judging speed and distance,

▸▸ a lack of concentration,

▸▸ social and emotional problems; e.g. low self-esteem, anxiety,

▸▸ weak muscle tone,

▸▸ disorganisation,

▸▸ difficulties with relationships,

▸▸ difficulties with maths,

▸▸ slow handwriting (failing to finish words off) and drawing, poor pen grip,

▸▸ difficulties with relationships.[10]

There is also some evidence that those who have Dyspraxia are more prone to certain medical conditions such as strokes.[11]

that they both stay on and work properly is an art. The rest of the family want variety in their meals and for some reason, yet to be explained, so much of what they want seems to involve much more food preparation than the individual can really cope with without becoming stressed!

<u>Cleaning teeth</u>
The area of personal hygiene can be one of the most troublesome areas if both gross-motor and fine-motor hand-based skills are affected. Hair care and dental hygiene in particular can be poor due to a combination of a number of difficulties that can be found with DCD/DD. One area of particular difficulty can be that of dental hygiene because it involves so many factors and skills. There may be difficulties in controlling the brush due to poor fine-motor control and/or poor spatial relationship skills. Individuals can also have difficulties in using the correct pressure. All of these difficulties can combine to cause individuals to hurt the inside of their mouths and/or make their gums bleed. Heightened oral sensitivity can cause them to dislike the texture of the brush and/or the feel of it in the mouth. Heightened awareness of taste and/or smell can cause them to dislike the smell/taste of the toothpaste. Difficulties in swallowing can cause them to 'gag' on the saliva/liquid that collects in the mouth whilst brushing. All of these factors can result in teeth being rarely/poorly cleaned and can make visits to the dentist very stressful, especially if individuals are also affected by 'hyperacusis' where they cannot cope with certain levels of sound; for example, dentist drills. A useful strategy is to clean the child's teeth using a very soft (baby's/infant) toothbrush and to find a flavour of toothpaste that the child can tolerate (or even just use a wet toothbrush). Dental gum and dental mouthwashes can also be useful in some cases.

Conditions that can be seen alongside motor coordination difficulties
A wide range of medical conditions are associated with Dyspraxia, such as epilepsy, hydrocephalus, Fragile-X (see Book 1), head injury, and Asperger's Syndrome (see Book 5). The latter comes within Autistic Spectrum Disorder, where individuals:

▸▸ have difficulties in communication (for example, Semantic-pragmatic disorder, see Book 4),

▸▸ have difficulties in social interactions,

▸▸ exhibit repetitive and stereotyped patterns of behaviour and restricted interests or activity (see Book 5).

Assessors need to be aware of some of the fairly rare medical conditions where motor coordination difficulties are one of the

Difficulties in knowing where to put the tongue and/or in controlling it whilst cleaning the teeth can cause problems in co-ordinating these movements plus those of the brush.

Dressing one's own or one's daughter's hair (e.g. in a ponytail) can be rather difficult. Some difficulties with hair care can be resolved (see page 27) though pony tails and bunches which both look alright and stay in are most probably asking a bit too much!

A dislike of having ones hair/nails touched and or cut is a commonly associated with Developmental Dyspraxia. This needs to be brought to the attention of all those who work with young children. The individual can also dislike doing any of these tasks for him/herself. Also see Book 5 and Chapter 2 of this book.

chief characteristics. Dr Amanda Kirby, in *Dyspraxia: the Hidden Handicap,* draws attention to two such conditions:

<u>Neurofibromatosis</u>
Characterised by the presence of at least ten pale or dark brown patches on the skin known as café au lait spots (of various sizes) and neurofibromas. The latter (firm or fleshy lumps under the skin) can be of various sizes. To see what these lumps and spots look like go to http://neurosurgery.mgh.harvard.edu/NFR/photos.htm The UK charity for this condition is at http: www.nfa.zetnet.co.uk

<u>Ehrlos Danlos Syndrome</u>
There are many different types of this condition. Skin may bruise more easily than normal, joints be more flexible than normal, velvety skin be seen, individuals tend to be clumsy, awkward and accident prone. Skin tends to be fragile (bruises/scars easily). Painful limbs may also be present. Learning difficulties are not normally associated with this condition. (Tel: 01748 82386, email: EDS-UK@compuserve.com)

Other Areas of difficulty
<u>Literacy difficulties</u> Difficulties in learning to read and/or spell may be present (see Books 3 and 4).

<u>Mathematical difficulties</u> A Specific Learning Difficulty in numeracy/mathematics is common amongst those who have Developmental Dyspraxia (see *Mathematics Solutions – An Introduction to Dyscalculia,* by Jan Poustie et al.).

<u>Attention Difficulties</u> Some individuals will also have difficulty in settling down to work (which may be associated with Attention Deficit Hyperactivity Disorder, see Book 5). They may need a few minutes at the beginning of the lesson to focus and calm down if they have had to rush to a previous lesson. This can also be linked to Metabolic Dysfunction (see Book 1).

Education and Dyspraxia/DCD
Parents and teachers can find the diagnosis of Developmental Dyspraxia/DCD traumatising and/or daunting. They, along with adults who have the condition) are likely to cope better if they have a 'working knowledge' of the condition, which the local Dyspraxia Foundation coordinator can provide. [12] (A useful book for children is *Dyscover Yourself* by Gill Dixon, published by the Dyspraxia Foundation), As the student's needs are so complex, the parents, teachers and students need to work together to identify key areas for concern and, in the case of school-age students, need to design both a long- and short-term Individual

Many teachers, confronted by a pile of reports on a child, may comment that the student is 'the most assessed child they have seen'. Teachers can find it difficult to accept that the student needs such a full assessment. Unfortunately, if a full assessment is not made, many pieces of the diagnostic 'jigsaw' will be missing and intervention is unlikely to be appropriate. It will thus be less effective. Teachers can also find the sheer volume of the reports too much to take in and feel that the child's needs are so complex that they cannot meet them.

Education Plan (IEP). Both perspectives are necessary, as it is easy to get 'bogged down' in short-term goals and forget that there is a bigger long-term picture. These IEPs will enable both parents and teachers to know what expectations they each have of the student.

Teachers of practical subjects especially need to be aware of the problems caused by DCD/DD, PE lessons and Sports Day in particular should not be the nightmare that so many of us remember long into adulthood.

Adulthood

For those of us who have DCD/DD the loss of self-esteem and self-confidence in physical tasks can make the individual feel inadequate and less likely to take part in physical leisure pursuits; e. g. keep fit classes. Poor presentation of self (via one's appearance and one's handwriting) can give totally the wrong impression about the individual. Eventually with support (or out of sheer determination) individuals can both accept and find ways around their DCD/DD if those around them also accept it. DCD/DD is part of the adult, in reality a small part but one which can become dominant if we let it do so. After all, in the great scheme of things the odd broken plate, the occasional burnt meal and the habit of sloppy dressing is not really that important - it is the person that matters not the clothes that we wear.

For those whose difficulties continue into adulthood, there is a need for a greater awareness of DCD/DD amongst employers. There is also the need for an effective support system whereby adults (with low-level to severe DCD/DD) can receive both training for their job and teaching to overcome their difficulties. This needs to be under a single long-term government-funded training initiative. Such individuals will need support from their partners if they are not always to feel inadequate in motor-based tasks which can range from DIY to cleaning the house. A useful resource is *Living with Dyspraxia: a guide for adults with developmental dyspraxia*, compiled by Mary Colley and the Dyspraxia Foundation Adult Support Group, ISBN 0 953434419.

References and footnotes

1. Dr Ian McKinlay.
2. Dr Ian McKinlay.
3. The writer has observed a child who has Dyspraxia wearing her jeans back to front without any apparent awareness of the discomfort she must have felt.
4. Dr Ian McKinlay.
5. Useful sources of information: *Watch me, I can do it* by Neralie Cocks, *Take Time* by Mary Nash-Wortham and Jean Hunt, and *Graded Activities for Children with Motor Difficulties* by James P. Russell.
6. Dr Ian McKinlay.
7. Dr Ian McKinlay at the Dyspraxia Foundation's conference *Theory into Practice* held on 13/14 September 2002.
8. A good source of information on this subject is *Perceptual Motor Difficulties*, by Dorothy Penso.
9. Mary Colley, of the Adult Dyspraxia helpline (Tel: 0207 435 5443).
10. Mary Colley, of the Adult Dyspraxia helpline (Tel: 0207 435 5443).
11. Information cited at the Dyspraxia Foundation's conference *Theory into Practice* (13/14 September 2002).
12. The British Dyslexia Association's local helpline and befriender may also be of use, Tel. 0118 966 8271.

Table 1
Those with Dyspraxia may have difficulties in playing games due to problems in understanding the rules. In such cases, these children can be perceived as being overly assertive, since they insist upon playing games based upon their own rules. Such children will often find it easier to play with pupils younger than themselves. (They can become isolated when they transfer to secondary school where there are no younger children to play with.) Also see Book 5.

PART 2 – Identifying

TABLE 1: Important indicators of Developmental Dyspraxia and their consequences

1. Poor balancing skills
Caused by motor planning difficulties, which can lead to problems in learning to ride a bike, rollerblade etc. Balancing skills can also be affected by the appropriate mechanism in the inner ear failing to register speed, orientation and direction of movement. Individuals may have travel sickness and dislike swings etc.

2. Difficulties in doing tasks that need good control over fingers (fine-motor control); for example:

a.   *Difficulties in getting dressed.* This includes difficulties in learning to cope with fastenings (for example, zips, buttons, buckles, shoelaces) and ties. This is mainly a fine-motor and sequencing difficulty and is generally termed Dressing Dyspraxia (which is a subgroup of Dyspraxia).

b.   *Difficulties in: writing, drawing, cutting.* May have difficulties in colouring-in shapes without going over the edge of the shape.

c.   *Difficulties with handling small objects.* Individuals may be able to pick up and move counters at speed with ease but find it difficult to manipulate objects; such as jigsaw pieces and construction toys. These sorts of difficulties can also be related to poor spatial skills.

d.   *Difficulties in using a knife, fork and spoon.*

3. Difficulties relating to spatial awareness and judging distances.
Children are not aware that a mug placed on the edge of a table is likely to be knocked over. They can misjudge stairs and so frequently fall down them, especially during a 'growth spurt' when they no longer know where the ends of their limbs are. Individuals can knock into people and misjudge gaps. Some with this problem have joint laxity.

4. Fidgeting
This may be caused by low muscle tone and Attention Deficit Hyperactivity Disorder. Some of these individuals have motor problems and vice versa. [1] *(These actions ARE NOT DELIBERATE. Such children have to exert a tremendous amount of control only to fidget just a little; to not fidget at all may be impossible.)* Some individuals that come within this category are defined as having DAMP Syndrome, where there is a combination of disorders of attention, motor coordination

and perception – see Book 5). Autistic Spectrum Disorder can also be seen as part of this Syndrome (see Book 5). Also see www.rcpsych.ac. uk/press/prelease/pr/pr_238.htm and www.timedoc.net/abstracts/ motor_skills.htm

5. Clumsiness
'Many have used clumsiness to describe motor learning difficulties – others use it to describe gaucheness or proneness to accidents.' [2]
This can also be seen as part of Autistic Spectrum Disorder (see Book 5). *Note: some of those who have DCD/DD are not clumsy!*

6. Sucking, swallowing, and chewing difficulties that may develop into speech articulation problems; for example, Verbal (Articulatory) and Oral Dyspraxia.

a. *Difficulties with the mechanics of swallowing.* Individuals may have difficulties in closing their mouth whilst eating (which can also be linked to poor breath control). They may have taken a long time to feed as a baby and some may still eat very slowly at secondary school. The 'first and second sitting' system in schools may not provide them with enough time to eat their lunch and so they may be hungry most of the afternoon. (Packed lunches will need to consist of easily chewed foods which they can eat quickly.) They may find it difficult to swallow catarrh when they have a cold. Also see Books 3 and 5.

b. *Difficulties with the mechanics of chewing.* Individuals may gulp food down without chewing it. If swallowing difficulties are present this group of individuals may eat very, very quickly.

c. *Slowness in learning to use a straw.*

d. *A preference for foods that need very little chewing.* This can also be related to textural/oral sensitivity.

7. Difficulties in learning to blow the nose
This can still prove difficult at secondary school, which can be very embarrassing if the individual has a cold or hay fever. Atopic conditions such as eczema, hay fever and asthma are believed by some professionals, such as Geschwind, to be more common in SpLD individuals.

8. Lack of coordination between the two sides of the body, with the individual often avoiding crossing the 'midline'
The 'midline' is a hypothetical vertical line passing through the middle of the body from top to bottom.

9. Associated features often seen are:

a. *Clinging, dependent behaviour;*
    wanting to be too close to people (so that they feel that

Difficulties in using cutlery is caused by several factors; for example, poor shoulder control means that individuals will tear food with the knife rather than cut it. Poor eye/ hand function results in messy eating, with food missing the mouth. Poor eye/hand control results in difficulty in controlling the utensils (food can end up on the table/floor and so can the utensils!). *Also see Bilateral Integration section on page 18.*

Learning to play a musical instrument can help students learn to cross the midline, see *Music Solutions* by Jan Poustie (ISBN 1901544 737).

Those with Dyspraxia may be bullied or may bully others
'Most children are teased and tormented at some time but their response varies according to the confidence and competence of the child.' (Dr Ian McKinlay). Also see Book 5.

their personal space is being invaded) and needing lots of cuddles.

b. *Over-reaction to temperature;*
also see Book 5; especially being unable to cope with hot and humid conditions, [3] may also not be able to cope with being cold.

c. *Dislike having hair cut/combed, or teeth brushed;*
though it should be noted that some individuals who have Dyspraxia find great pleasure in having their hair touched.

d. *Emotional problems;*
'anxiety, depression and withdrawal being the commonest ones.' [4]

e. *Behaviour inappropriate to the situation;*
This can take several forms; e.g. they can:

➠ have difficulties in controlling their emotions,

➠ be bullied by their peer group and/or they bully others.

References to Table 1
1, 2, 4. Dr Ian McKinlay
3. Dr Sidney Chu in *'Praxis makes Perfect 1'*

TABLE 2 : Sensory perception difficulties

1. **'Tactile defensiveness and hypersensitivity** are associated with a minority of those who have Dyspraxia. (The need for reassurance, clinging etc. reflects the majority).' [1] These aspects of Dyspraxia can be seen as:

   a. *Over-reaction to certain smells* (feeling physically ill at some smells and over-elated by others). Also see Book 5.

   b. *A dislike of being touched* (including being tickled) and/or being in crowds. Also see Book 5.

   c. *A dislike of having hair cut/combed, teeth brushed, or nails cut.*

   d. *Over-reaction to taste and textures.* The latter can include the textures of clothing, towels etc.) and can be present as oral sensitivity with regard to both textures of food and anything else that goes into the mouth. Oral sensitivity can cause problems with maintaining dental hygiene, and this, along with a sensitivity to sound (hyperacusis – see Book 3), can make visits to the dentist exceptionally unpleasant. Also see Book 5.

Some individuals will have difficulties in settling down to work (which may be associated with Attention Deficit Hyperactivity Disorder). They may need a few minutes at the beginning of the lesson to focus and calm down if they have had to rush to be on time.

2. Difficulties in finding things against a busy background;
for example, difficulties in finding a certain pair of socks in a drawer full of underwear, or in spotting a word on the page. This problem should not be confused with that of the normal male who has difficulties in finding items in a cupboard because males have a narrower peripheral vision than females (see *Why men don't listen and women can't read maps* by A and B Pease, Pub. Pease Training International). In its severest form, this will cause the pupil to try to read the 'white bits' on the page rather than the black letters. Such pupils will need specialist intervention in order to be able to learn to read.

References to Table 2
1.   Dr Ian McKinlay.

TABLE 3: (Areas usually assessed by a paediatric physiotherapist)

1. Gross-motor functioning
The following areas will be assessed in relation to general posture: muscle power, symmetry of movements and agility. If this is poor, then you can expect the student to have considerable difficulties in maintaining a posture and, in consequence, to be moving from one position to another even whilst sitting. If the pupil's muscle tone or joints are lax (weak) then individuals are likely to have difficulty in applying the correct pressure to items. Thus they could break a test tube because they are having to hold it very tightly in order to control it. 'There are several common connective tissue laxity conditions, with increased risk of arthritis, poor healing of scars, uterine/rectal prolapse; these can occur alongside coordination problems.' [1] General posture includes joint range and laxity, muscle tone, muscle power, symmetry of movements and agility plus the following:
a. *Shoulder control:* this relates to muscle strength and joint laxity around the shoulder girdle. It is an important factor for hand function and a prerequisite for being able to write. [2]
b. *Pelvic control:* this relates to the joint laxity around the hips and is required for activities such as standing on one leg, hopping and kicking a ball. [3]
c. *Proximal stability:* the ability to use both shoulder and pelvic control together.
d. *Balance:* this involves the trunk muscles, which bend, straighten

Balance difficulties may be seen in the playground when children can be knocked over by peers running past them. Children with balance problems may also find sitting still on a chair difficult and various PE tasks may be very hard; for example, balancing on a narrow object.

A useful and fun piece of apparatus for developing balance skills is *The Wobbler* (Tel. 01884 841305).

Visual-motor integration
Poor hand/eye coordination will cause difficulties in using small apparatus; for example, needle and thread, science equipment, paintbrush, pen and compass.

References to Table 3

1 and 9. Dr Ian McKinlay.

2- 8 and 10. Lee M. and French J.: *Dyspraxia – A Handbook for Therapists* (pub. by APCP Publications, 1994).

and rotate the body, in addition to the shoulder and pelvic control. Good balance is important in all positions; for example, sitting, kneeling and standing; in order to maintain the position and not be easily taken off it or knocked over.

2. Other related areas which may be assessed

a) Eye/hand coordination

This is the ability of the eyes and hands to work together, and is needed for activities such as writing, throwing and catching a ball. [4] It is mainly assessed by the physiotherapist with ball activities which involve the individual in one- and two-handed throwing and catching.

b) Eye/foot coordination

This is the ability of the eyes and feet to work together and is required for walking around obstacles, over rough surfaces or up and down stairs. [5] Assessment of this area will include kicking and trapping a kicked ball.

c) Motor planning

This is the ability to plan the necessary movements that are required to move from one position to another. Individuals with planning difficulties often show problems with task organisation and writing essays. [6]

d) Symmetrical integration

This is the ability to move both sides of the body simultaneously in identical patterns of movement such as jumping forwards. [7] Difficulties in this area are likely to cause problems in learning to swim.

e) Bilateral integration

This is the ability to move both sides of the body simultaneously in opposing patterns of movement, such as in jumping sideways. This is particularly important in assessing whether the child has difficulty with activities such as using a knife and fork. [8]

3. Additional areas which will also be assessed (some of which will be formally recognised by an Educational Psychologist)

a) Short-term visual and verbal memory

This is the ability to remember activities that are both shown to, and asked of, the student. These tasks are required for activities such as copying from the blackboard and taking/writing dictation.

b) Directional awareness

The student may not understand the terms forwards, backwards, sideways and diagonally (or may not be able accurately to plan and execute the relevant movements).

c) Right- and left-side side dominance:

For example, whether the individual uses the right or left hand/foot/eye most of the time. If the dominance is 'unfixed', the individual might use the right hand one minute and the left the next. 'If the dominance is not established until late (for example, after seven years for writing) this can cause difficulties with practical tasks.' [9]

d) Body perception and proprioception: *(also see Table 4).*

This includes body image, body scheme and body awareness.

e) The ability to cross the midline. *(See page 15.)*

f) Kinaesthetic awareness

The ability of the brain to know the position and movements of parts of the body. [10]

g) Rhythm and timing

This is taken into account in all activities.

h) Auditory and visual motor sequencing

For example, clapping out a tune or copying movements when shown to the child. Also see Book 3.

i) Sensory perception

Recognition of when one is being touched and the ability to recognise an object by touch alone.

j) Distractibility and concentration skills *(also see Books 1 and 5).*

TABLE 4 (Areas usually assessed by a paediatric occupational therapist. Those marked with 'p' may be assessed by a paediatric physiotherapist.)

1. Motor

a) Motor proficiency (p)

Weakness in upper limb coordination is likely to cause problems in controlling bats/racquets in PE and apparatus in science, DT and art lessons. Problems in controlling the apparatus in handwriting, and in playing musical instruments may also be seen. See Chapter 2 and *Music Solutions,* second edition, by Jan Poustie, ISBN 1 901544 73 7.

b) Visual-motor integration

Visual-motor control difficulties cause problems in knowing where to place apparatus/parts of the body in order to carry out a task correctly. Poor hand/eye coordination will cause difficulties in using small apparatus; e.g. needle and thread,

Table 4: sensory aspects

Visual perception  Assessment includes the individual's ability to judge trajectories of moving objects and relative speeds. This is a vital skill for drivers and cyclists. Individuals with difficulties in this area may take longer to learn to drive and are likely to tire more easily when driving/riding a bike. Such children will need support when learning to judge the trajectories of balls, and the relative distance of bikes and cars and it will take them longer to learn to cross roads safely.

The pupil may write his/her letters so small that they give an impression of neatness (and inaccuracies of construction are not spotted at a glance) but s/he cannot control the pen enough to make the letters any larger (also see Chapter 2).

The pupil may write his/her letters so small that they give an impression of neatness (and inaccuracies of construction are not spotted at a glance) but s/he cannot control the pen enough to make the letters any larger (also see Chapter 2).

science equipment, paint brush, pen and compass. See Chapter 2.

c) <u>Motor planning difficulties (p)</u>

d) <u>Muscle tone and strength (p)</u>

Tremor can be apparent in some individuals. It can have a variety of causes, one of which is a difficulty in regulating the amount of pressure used to control an object; this can lead to 'tremor' of the hand. Sometimes this is not apparent when the individual is not joining the letters, but becomes very apparent when s/he is asked to join them. In such cases, it is the increased effort that heightens the difficulty. This is one of many factors that may cause the individual to press very hard. (Knuckles will whiten when writing and the imprint of the writing can be seen on the next page, or pages, of a notepad.) This will result in the individual finding writing both painful and tiring. Poor control of pressure can cause individuals to grip objects so hard that they break or lose control of them. Poor muscle tone can be shown by poor posture, that is slouching over a desk and round shoulders. Such individuals will tire more easily because they are working harder to stay upright.

If the individual's shoulder girdle is weak s/he will have difficulty in activities that involve shoulder actions. These include writing on paper and writing on the blackboard. Students may have difficulties in playing instruments that need to be supported and/ or held at shoulder height (for example, instruments in a marching band, or violins and flutes). (Also see page 7.)

e) <u>Eye movements</u>

Problems in controlling eye movements are part of what is called by some Visual or Occulomotor Dyspraxia, and, by others, Near-vision Dysfunctioning. Such difficulties will affect the quality and quantity of written work and learning to read. They will also affect any work where fine control of objects is required; such as threading needles or accurately measuring on analogue scales. When visual difficulties are present, individuals will need to keep their place by using their finger/pencil/book mark when reading. The control needed for this task, combined with the visual difficulties can be too great for some individuals with both difficulties. (See Dyslexia and Meares-Irlen Syndrome, Books 1 and 4.)

f) <u>Cognition (Learning Behaviours)</u>

These include behaviours such as concentration, problem solving, sequencing, memory, listening skills, planning and organisation, initiation (being able to start a task), motivation, perseveration (not being able to stop the task/train of thought) and generalisation (being able to take a learned behaviour/skill and use it in a different setting).

The above behaviours are determined by clinical observation based upon medical/paramedical training and clinical experience and the use of checklists. (Some authorities have their own checklists whilst other assessments include them as part of the scoring criteria.) This may lead to the therapist referring the individual to another professional for diagnosis and/or the introduction of strategies to overcome the difficulties.

2. Sensory aspects

a) Visual perception
Different aspects of this area will be assessed, depending upon the age of the individual and the assessment tool; for example, visual discrimination, visual memory, visual figure-ground, visual closure and depth perception. A referral may be necessary to eliminate the need for glasses as a cause of visual problems prior to diagnosing visual perceptual difficulties. (Also see page 19 of this book and Book 4 Near-vision Dysfunctioning.)

b) Body spatial awareness
The ability to work out one's position in relation to the rest of the world, and also the relationship of one's limbs to each other; (i.e. right from left and directional confusion).

c) Listening skills
How the individual copes with listening tasks within the classroom. This is assessed by talking to the teacher, parent and individual and by observation during the assessment.

d) Touch, smell and taste sensitivity
Within the classroom situation, the most important of these is touch. (Teachers need to note that smell sensitivity can cause difficulties in foot technology/cookery lessons. Taste/touch sensitivity can result in faddy eaters.) Touch sensitivity may be evident in individuals who do not like such activities as contact sports or being jostled in a queue. Such individuals may find such things as a teacher's (or work colleague's) pat on the back or hand guiding his/her own hand when writing, uncomfortable (see Book 7). Some individuals may dislike the feel of certain writing implements, such as wax crayons. Other individuals crave being touched.

e) Proprioception
This is the sense of knowing where your body's limbs are and where the limbs are moving to in space. The latter is also known as kinaesthesia. This will be assessed in discussion with a teacher or individual about their performance in physical education and sport. It also concerns the very fine movements that are carried

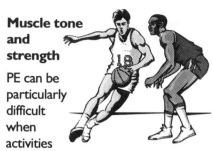

Muscle tone and strength

PE can be particularly difficult when activities involve shoulders as the controlling force. However, some of those who have DCD/DD do find some sports easier to learn than others; e.g. those sports where the ball travels close to the ground such has hockey and football.

For details of recommended reading books see page 49.

out automatically during writing (e.g. the eye is not controlling all the movements of the hand but the muscles of the hand remember what to do – kinaesthetic memory). All of these factors are also assessed through clinical observation of the individual carrying out various tasks.

f) Balance (vestibular) skills

Vestibular skills refer to an awareness of the speed, orientation and direction of movement. Problems in this area may lead to travel sickness, poor saving reactions during a fall, and poor balance reactions when walking on a beam. In serious cases, individuals may have difficulty in getting down on to the floor and problems in feeling comfortable lying on their back.

PART 3 - Referring

For methods and types of assessment used by different professionals, see Appendix 1, page 45

Referring for areas of functioning found in Tables 1 – 4

Either the school or the parents can ask the school doctor or the GP to refer the child for DCD/DD. This professional may refer the child to a paediatrician or directly to *paediatric physio/occupational therapists* for an assessment of fine and gross motor (including Graphomotor Dyspraxia and other writing difficulties) sensory and cognitive (thinking) skills. Some educational professionals have the expertise to assess for DCD/DD too. Note: secondary school aged students and adults may find it difficult to obtain an assessment as professionals such as Paediatric Occupational Therapists tend to focus on the younger aged children.

Verbal (Articulatory) Dyspraxia

A speech and language therapist (SLT) assessment is necessary whereby a thorough assessment of expressive and receptive language function is conducted (e.g. through the use of the Celf-R assessment tool) plus any problems with the production of speech are also determined. The parents of the child can either:

➼ Contact their GP and ask him to refer them to the SLT.

➼ Make a parental referral by contacting their local NHS hospital's speech and language department and ask for a referral form which they then complete and send back to the department.

Oral Dyspraxia: Use the same referral process as for Verbal Dyspraxia.

Occulomotor Dyspraxia: see Book 4 of this library.

Graphomotor Dyspraxia: see page 39 of this book.

CHAPTER 2
Identifying handwriting difficulties

PART 1 – Understanding

Writing is used for a great variety of tasks, some of which can be performed slowly (for example, writing one's signature, filling in forms), whilst others (such as answering examination questions and taking notes) require speed. The field of writing difficulties is one in which there appears to be many strongly held views as to its various causes, valid types of assessment and the means by which the difficulties can be overcome. This is because it is a very complex field where many, if not all, of the conditions found within the SpLD Profile meet and/ or are reflected. It is further complicated because our knowledge of many of its aspects is still minimal due to the limited amount of research in this field as compared with that of literacy research. As a result of the above, together with conditions/circumstances that can affect writing skills, we have a situation in the UK where, by Year 3, many children need extra handwriting tuition [1] and, by secondary school, far too many experience pain when they write. [2] Once into adulthood, the unrecognised need for tuition (and the pain when writing) may lead to individuals failing to fulfil their potential. In more severe cases, the pain may affect manual control of objects. [3]

Few of us escape the need to write. Despite modern technology, 'handwriting is still an essential skill. People present themselves to the world through their handwriting, and are inevitably judged by it.' [4] However, handwriting is quickly becoming a less essential skill in the workplace, where computers now dominate as the means of recording information. The opposite is true in education. Education is therefore requiring something of children that will not be required of them in the workplace. The sooner education catches up with the non-educational world the better, as only then will all of our students be enabled to use computers as their main means of recording.

There are many different 'ways' of writing. Each 'way' will make different demands upon the individual's body and his or her cognitive processes. Some will make considerable demands on motor skills and require good posture; for example, writing information by hand (handwriting) and the art of calligraphy. Others are less demanding; for example, typing (especially with an ergonomic keyboard) and dictation via a tape recorder (though the latter does need good control of the organs of speech and the ability to think/process information whilst speaking). Of all these tasks, handwriting is the one that the majority of us do the most.

Handwriting difficulties are not a recent problem!
'My handwriting looks as if a swarm of ants, escaping from an ink bottle, had walked over a sheet of paper without wiping their legs.'
(Sydney Smith, 1772–1845)

Nowadays, when writing creatively one has quickly to both process information and write. For many individuals, that can be hard work, tiring and in many cases painful, but for those with writing difficulties it can be an extremely hard, or, even impossible task.

The body's apparatus for writing is being put under intensive pressure as a result of text messaging, handheld games and the education system's demand for huge quantities of handwritten work as proof of knowledge. As a result the body (especially the fingers and wrist) is put under so much strain that tendonitis and RSI can develop. All schools should have a writing policy which limits the amount of handwriting that their students have to do each day.

Have we been writing more, and faster, since the nineteenth century?

Yes! In the nineteenth century one of the main requirements of handwriting was a very neat script that could easily be read by others; for example, copperplate (in which accuracy was more important than speed). [5] With the huge upsurge in information during the twentieth century, there came a need to both read and write more and therefore increase speed. Consequently, new equipment appeared, such as the word processor and new writing styles and pens also appeared. Thus, the old-fashioned sloping desk, which kept the writing hand at a good angle for writing, has been replaced by modern desks/tables which are flat. Copperplate and the quill kept writing speed slow, whilst modern styles and pens allow one to write faster. Therefore it would seem likely that the needs of the individual may have been sacrificed in order to meet society's need for speed and quantity. In the past, many people may well have been able easily to process information whilst writing at their fastest possible speed.

The sheer volume of writing required from students in educational establishments can be overwhelming. In schools, one of the requirements of the National Curriculum of England and Wales for English at Key Stage 2 is that in writing 'pupils should be given opportunity to plan, draft and improve their work on paper and on screen'. [6] This puts even more demands upon weak handwriting skills and has resulted in some teachers having concerns about providing enough *evidence of attainment*. Thus, some children are being required to write most tasks two or three times rather than using less handwriting-intensive ways of planning/writing (for example, mind mapping and word-processing).

Are there any easy writing tasks?

Not really; some may appear to be exceptionally easy but in reality they are the opposite. For example, consider the following statement:

> Copying from the blackboard – that's the easiest task I give my pupils (Year-3 teacher)

Blackboard copying is actually a very complex task. It requires memory, mechanical writing, visual and perceptual skills (including the ability to scan text over a very large area to see where you are on the board), and the ability to stay on task. Individuals with Near-vision Dysfunctioning and/or perceptual difficulties are likely to have considerable problems. Thus, those who have problems with releasing focus will be in a situation where the whole world appears out of focus for a great deal of the time. This is because their eyes fail to adapt to the changing focus involved in repeatedly looking up (long distance) and looking down (short distance). *(See Books 1 and 4.)* Individuals who have severe Attention Deficit Disorder *(see Book 5)*, severe memory difficulties *(see Book 5)* or severe near-vision and/or perceptual difficulties *(see Book 4)* or a milder combination of two or three of them are likely to find the task too hard, and alternatives will need to be found. [7]

How do specialists regard difficulties in handwriting?

The difficulties appear to be regarded in three main ways at present:

1. As usually being indicators of other problems, such as insecure spelling, stress, short-sightedness, incorrect posture. [8]

2. As being a motor planning and organisational difficulty, which can be present as part of DCD/DD.

3. As commonly being an indicator of any, or several, of the conditions that come within the SpLD Profile.

Stress often accompanies the conditions found within the SpLD Profile [10] and a person can have more than one of the conditions. Writing requires a combination of skills, the acquisition of which could be affected by various factors (including those conditions found within the SpLD Profile). Therefore all of the above views are valid though all may not be represented in each individual.

What term can we use when a motor planning and organisational difficulty is the cause of writing problems?

The term used for this difficulty in some countries (such as Holland) is Dysgraphia, but this term is not currently in use in the UK and is disliked by many. [11] It is also a slightly ambiguous term, as it can be used as a general term to describe a condition where there are difficulties within the writing process due to slowed (or delayed) development of any of the skills needed for writing (such as verbal skills, spelling, writing). [12] As a result, professionals will use all sorts of terms for this difficulty with perhaps Dyspraxia and/or a specific learning difficulty in fine-motor planning and organisation being the more common ones. Neither of these terms really define the problem – Dyspraxia is too wide a term, as gross-motor function may only be minimally affected. Also, just because there is a difficulty in fine-motor control of the hand, it does not mean that other fine-motor skills are affected.

A failure with the teaching practice

The teacher may lack the knowledge base to teach handwriting well, to recognise an individual's difficulties and to remediate them as they occur. *(There are now some teachers in schools who received very little instruction in the teaching of handwriting during their teacher-training course.)* There is also evidence that each teacher will interpret the school model in slightly different ways, and this can create confusion in the child. [9]

Using a computer for the whole task (planning, draft, editing and final copy) saves a great deal of time and frustration for the student when handwriting/planning and organisational difficulties are present.

Identification Solutions for Coordination Difficulties by Jan Poustie   ISBN 1 901544 87 7

The underlying causes of Graphomotor Dyspraxia can affect so many activities that they can have a considerable effect not just on the individual's writing but on the life of the individual at school, work and at home. Research indicates that 10% of children have the condition and that there are no significant differences in its incidence between left- and right-handers. [13]

Certain other fine-motor-based subgroups of Dyspraxia had already been more accurately named by placing an identifier before the word Dyspraxia; for example, Occulomotor Dyspraxia and Verbal (also known as Articulatory) Dyspraxia. Since the word graphomotor can be used to describe the creation of an image/letter on a surface, (such as paper) the author (in 1997) invented the term Graphomotor Dyspraxia. This term both describes the difficulty and the condition of which it is a part, and can be used more closely to define a writing difficulty where:

1. *There are difficulties in fine-motor planning and organisation and control relating to the hand, which may range from barely noticeable to severe.* (Similar difficulties in gross-motor skills relating to the arm/shoulder and postural movements are also likely to be present, but will also range from barely noticeable to severe.)

2. *'Constructional Dyspraxia' may also be present.* This will show itself as a difficulty in accurately representing the spatial relations of letters/words (for example, words too close to each other; letters misaligned).

3. *The causes of the difficulties mentioned at 1 and 2 above have been present since birth.*

How does Graphomotor Dyspraxia affect everyday skills?
The difficulties that occur as a result of Graphomotor Dyspraxia, and the sensitivities that can be associated with Dyspraxia, are often noticeable in the area of hair care. A reluctance to comb one's hair can thus be due to difficulties with controlling the comb/brush due to poor fine-motor control and/or poor spatial relationship skills. If the individual also uses incorrect pressure, or has scalp sensitivity (which makes the 'feel' of the comb/brush unpleasant) then it is not surprising that s/he avoids the task and does not wish the parent to do it either.

An overview of writing difficulties
There is no doubt that moderate to severe writing difficulties (whatever their underlying reason) are a cause for concern. For many of us working in this field, the writing of someone with severe Graphomotor Dyspraxia leaves little doubt that a specific writing difficulty exists.

It is those who have low to moderate levels of writing difficulties that are likely to be unrecognised. It takes much

Identification Solutions for Coordination Difficulties by Jan Poustie   ISBN 1 901544 87 7

more control to join letters, and so the habit of not joining (which is becoming quite common at secondary-school level in many countries) [13] can hide some of the signs of writing difficulties. If both reading and writing are poor, the student may be regarded as being less able. (This is more likely if s/he only uses a very small vocabulary in written work because that is all that s/he has a chance of spelling.) The individual may be criticised for being lazy and/or careless and for not finishing his/her work fast enough. It is not realised that s/he is, in fact, has several conditions that come within the Specific Learning Difficulty Profile. Writing difficulties become more difficult to recognise if the individual writes very little, which s/he may achieve by avoiding writing tasks. The child may misbehave/volunteer for tasks to get out of the classroom, write hardly anything at all whilst going into a daydream to escape from the problem, or write very neatly but very slowly (often pressing very hard). The adult, of course, can conveniently forget items such as his/her glasses and pen and/or be forced to take a job that requires very little writing.

The increased demands on handwriting skills as individuals progress through their education may highlight motor planning and control difficulties that were manageable when there were less demands being made upon them. A slow writing speed usually becomes a noticeable problem for school children when they are seven years old, as this is when the emphasis starts to change from practical to written work. Often, these are the children who have to stay in at breaks to complete their work. At this level, the classroom walls may have many examples of 'neat' versions of writing-based tasks. In some schools, such work may have been handwritten three times; that is plan, draft, neat and then typed on to the computer. Such a process is extremely time-consuming and puts tremendous pressure on the child's writing skills.

By the time individuals reach secondary school, writing can be a major problem. In some schools, there is still a concentration on using handwriting intensively for copying, proving knowledge, note-taking and creative writing. The individual may just about be able to survive the amount of written work during the day but cannot face homework requirements, so, s/he will either fail to bring in the work on time, submit incomplete work, or just not hand it in at all. By the age of thirteen, some may no longer be able to read their own writing all of the time (especially when they are trying to take down rushed homework

Scalp sensitivity can make it particularly difficult for girls who can find any means of tying back long hair; e.g. bunches, pony tails painful. A different textured brush and short hair can help!

Case study: Oliver

Oliver had just left secondary school. He found it painful when he had to handwrite more than one sentence. Discussion with him revealed that in his last two weeks at school he had written continuously for every lesson.

Just as we require our students to use joined-up writing in school so our schools need some 'joined-up thinking' when it comes to handwriting. All schools need to adopt a handwriting policy that limits the amount of handwriting done by its students during a school day. The policy should ensure that no student has two lessons in a row where the production of handwritten work is the main task. We should not demand more from children than we, as adults, are prepared to do. Most educators find their hands are tired after just trying to take notes in a one-hour lecture.

instructions that are given at the end of a lesson). If this situation is not resolved by the GSCE years, these individuals may not be able to show their true ability in either their assignments and/or their examinations.

Criticism of a person's work achieves little. Affected students do not need anyone to tell them how messy their work is, they already know – but what they do not know is the strategies by which this can be improved. The only result of criticism is loss of self-esteem and the deterioration of the relationship between the educator (or workplace manager) and the individual.

Instead of criticism, individuals need both an accurate diagnosis of their difficulties plus an appropriate programme to enable the difficulties to be overcome. Such a programme will need to include ways in which they can show their knowledge and ability (without the need for writing all of the time). It will also include activities that will improve the standard of writing; for example, exercises that help to strengthen weak muscles, activities to improve motor planning and teaching better letter construction. Other problems that could be causing (or contributing towards the difficulty) will also need to be recognised and resolved, such as spelling, language, visual difficulties, stress. Finally, the adoption of alternative strategies to writing, such as Mind Maps™ will be needed to reduce the quantity, whilst improving the quality, of the individual's written output. [14] (In schools and colleges this will benefit both the teacher and students as the former will have much less marking to do and the latter will have more time for learning and less strain on the writing arm.) By these means, we can help individuals to gain qualifications and jobs that reflect their true abilities, and so enable them to reach their potential in adulthood.

The high incidence of pain experienced by children when writing (especially that which is found in high achievers) [15] is evidence that our young people are not able to cope with the writing demands placed upon them. Soon we may all be in the same position – too much to write and not enough time to write it in. If we, as a society, are going to continue to make ever-increasing demands upon our student's writing skills then we may need to adjust our attitude to handwriting. This may involve changing the way in which we teach handwriting (including writing models and implements) and a re-evaluation of the tasks for which a handwritten script is required. It is also likely that we will need to look increasingly at alternative strategies to handwriting, including that of word processing.

It is already noticeable that there has arisen a wide divide between the school and the workplace with regard to the quality of equipment and the use of information technology. As a result of too little money being available to buy modern stock, this divide is increasing. The fact that many of our teachers still only have the most basic computer skills and little access to computers in the workplace (and maybe even less access to a printer or the internet) does not help the situation either. Too many educational establishments are the dumping ground for out-of-date (or slightly upgraded) equipment that companies have given away (or sold cheap) effectively becoming museums for machines bought in the late twentieth century that are fast passing their 'use by' dates. Much of this hardware has antiquated systems/programs that are difficult to use and thus do little to boost the confidence of teachers/trainers who may already feel inadequate in their use of computers. Such hardware is unable to operate the superb modern word-processing programs, text readers, predictive lexicons, typing tutors and voice-dictation systems that are now available and that could make life so much simpler for students with writing difficulties. [16] The lack of experience at secondary level of modern programs that are commonly found in the workplace (and on the home computer) creates yet more problems. It does not enable work started at school to be finished at home, or vice versa. Neither does this situation enable the individual to effect a smooth transition of computer-based skills from the educational environment into the workplace.

If difficulties remain unrecognised and unsupported into adulthood, the individual may find filling in forms such an obstacle to employment that a job is difficult to obtain. Those who gain work may have to refuse promotion because they know that they will not be able to cope with the writing requirement that a higher post entails unless a computer is provided for them.

Case study: Frederick

Frederick was thirteen years old when he was referred to the author because his Year-8 report was so damning that both he and parents were very distressed and worried. At this point, he could no longer read his own writing. He had a history of difficulties in learning to spell. His reading comprehension was found to be above his chronological age and his spelling was three years below chronological age. He was learning the violin but had experienced problems in learning to sight read and in finger control. His non-verbal IQ was found to be 125+ so this was a very bright young man. Dyspraxia (Oral, Graphomotor and Occulomotor) was identified by the tutor and later confirmed by other specialists. When just the first page of Gill Cotterell's phonic test was used he made 56 percent errors so his phonological knowledge was clearly very poor. (The test is part of *The Phonic Reference File*, published by LDA Learning, Tel: 01945 463444.) The author recommended that Frederick be enabled to use a computer for much of his work and that he be provided with a *Franklin* spellchecker.

Case study: Frederick Yr 8 report
General comment: "You obviously recognise that your presentation does need attention."
Maths: "There is a need for you to improve the presentation of your work. This is essential if you are to demonstrate clearly the high level of your understanding."
Science: Your presentation does need some attention."

Identification Solutions for Coordination Difficulties by Jan Poustie   ISBN 1 901544 87 7

For details of apparatus and books which may be useful when handwriting difficulties are present see page 49.

Comorbidity (conditions being seen alongside each other) is something that has been talked about in the last few years. Frederick's range of difficulties (having both Dyspraxia and Dyslexia) meant that the only way to teach him was to take into account his Dyspraxia, as this condition underlay his literacy problems. The period of tuition lasted two terms. The author used a phonological teaching approach to this student, and also taught dictionary skills and improved his writing. (If only this student had been taught to read and spell phonologically from the start he would have had no, or few, problems in these areas.) Initially, he progressed at normal speed. However, by the second term he was able to cover a vast amount of work in a one-hour lesson; for example, learning between three and four new sound patterns and doing pronunciation work, dictionary/vocabulary work and writing patterns. The author used two strategies to develop Frederick's reading and spelling skills. The first strategy focused on doing this by improving his pronunciation skills (see Book 3 for details) and the second achieved this by focusing on writing-skill improvement. The latter was achieved in the following way.

Upon looking at Frederick's writing it was found that three letters were causing most of the problem: 'x', 'f' and 's'. He was shown various handwriting models (letter styles) of these letters. Then, using the handwriting model that he liked best. he was taught the phonic patterns that used these letters. The patterns were written on a piece of lined paper by the author (using the new style for the 'x', 'f' and 's' and keeping the writing as identical as possible to Frederick's for the remaining letters.) Then, a clear overhead projector (OHP) acetate sheet was placed over the lined paper. Frederick wrote over the tutor's writing using an OHP pen – this meant that there was no resistance to the hand when he wrote, which made it much easier for him to learn the correct movements. Using the exercises found in *Watch Me, I Can Do It* (ISBN 0 7318 0578 X), by Neralie Cocks, Frederick was given a course of exercises to strengthen his low muscle tone and weak shoulder girdle, which were largely responsible for his writing difficulties. Virtually all teachers complained about how untidy he was except for his mathematics and science teachers who could see that, despite his presentation of work, he had what it takes to gain high qualifications in these subjects. Even though his mother was a Special Needs Governor of the school, there was still very little support being offered her son. Once the school received a specialist report from the author, they reluctantly made an appointment for Frederick to see an Educational Psychologist. It backed up everything that the author's report said, including both his range of difficulties and his level of intelligence.

This case shows the difficulty of providing provision that is acceptable to the student (in primary school, it is so much easier). At the age of thirteen, students may start tuition with great reluctance – their parents want their child to receive help but the student may rather ignore the problem. Frederick accepted the need to improve (and modify his writing) simply because he could no longer read it. By using writing as the main vehicle for his phonics tuition the author enabled Frederick to improve his reading and spelling skills as well as his writing. By the end of tuition he, and everyone else, could read his writing.

Frederick was adamant that he would not give up his lunch time for tuition as this was when he played football (which he was good at) with the other boys. He did not want to be withdrawn from lessons (as he would then stand out from the crowd). For him the only possible option was to provide tuition after school at times that suited him. As he was already receiving private lessons for his music, and also happened to know the author socially, he was quite happy to attend the lessons, as his peer group were unaware that they were happening.

Some of the teachers were interested in his out-of-school provision. His science teacher used to incorporate some of the techniques taught to Frederick (for example, Mind Mapping™) into his lessons and so recognised the value of such techniques for all of his students, not just Frederick.

Frederick's case shows how the needs of the parents have to be met as well as those of the student. He was ready to leave specialist tuition six weeks before he did so. However, his mother was very reluctant for the teaching to finish. Part of each of these final lessons was spent in enabling the mother to realise that her son would now be able to reach his potential. She needed to be convinced that she (having both an excellent relationship with her son and being a college lecturer herself) would be able to take him through his GCSEs. Frederick gained four 'A's and four 'B's at GCSE, which enabled him to move on to sixth Form College, where he was immediately seen by Special Needs staff. He was reassessed so that decisions could be made regarding the provision he would require for university. The presentation of his work in mathematics was helped by him using squared paper for both his GCSE and 'A' Level maths. This enabled him to keep his figures in line and thus to make less errors.

Frederick's case makes one wonder whether we are going about withdrawal lessons in the wrong way for some of our students (especially our teenagers). There would seem to be a case for such lessons to be offered in the evenings in a non-school setting.

Identification Solutions for Coordination Difficulties by Jan Poustie   ISBN 1 901544 87 7

At the start of tuition, Frederick's self-esteem was quite low, as were his life goals. He found it a great struggle to write just half a page of text. By the end of tuition, he was able to write double that amount without undue strain. He had started a touch-typing course and his school allowed him to use classroom-based computers for his written work. His parents were able to buy him a computer for homework too. However, not all students are happy using a computer at school. Some Dyspraxia/DCD students become social outcasts in the classroom and playground because of their inadequacies. When these students are given laptop computers they may fear (and experience) further social rejection (through comments and looks from their peer group when using it) and so will avoid using the computer. Such students may desperately need to use the laptop but they do need good support from staff to enable them to do so.

He achieved a B and two C's at 'A' Level in Chemistry, Biology and Mathematics and then went on to Warwick University. He applied for the Disabled Student's Allowance, was assessed for his IT needs and was provided with a computer, spellchecker, dictaphone and relevant software. He is now in his second year reading chemistry and is expected to achieve a 2:1 degree (which is only just below a first).

Frederick's tuition and support enabled him to raise his career goals. Prior to his tuition his goals were limited to the world he knew and to what he thought he could achieve. Thus, his initial desire to be an Exmoor Warden was based on him knowing that he could achieve this career with the minimum of academic achievements. Such a career could be based upon the excellent countryside skills that he had acquired thanks to his family's interest in the outdoor life. (These skills were so advanced that at thirteen he led a Ten Tors team over Dartmoor - one of the most challenging outdoor tasks that young people can do). However, once specialist intervention had occurred Frederick started to raise his sights from the safe world that he knew to more distant horizons. Now he is considering a possible career in industrial chemistry and furthering his academic qualifications (hopefully progressing to a master's degree).

PART 2 – Identifying

The relationship between skills needed for writing and the conditions found within the SpLD Profile
The conditions found within the Profile can affect the skills needed to achieve motor planning. Motor planning is a three-stage process involving mechanical, cognitive, visual and perceptual skills. (The individual has to come up with the idea, develop the plan of action and execute the movement for it.)

1. The mechanics of writing; that is the integration of muscle movements and sensory feedback.
When the cause of an individual's writing difficulty involves motor planning and organisation plus perceptual difficulties, then s/he may be described as having Dyspraxia. In such cases, gross-motor coordination problems will not always be present. Some individuals may only have Graphomotor Dyspraxia and some of the more subtle perceptual problems that can be seen alongside other fine and/or gross motor based forms of Dyspraxia; for example, touch and auditory sensitivity (see page 16).

2. Cognitive skills; for example, planning and organisation, problem solving, sequencing and memory.

Each type of writing task makes different demands upon the individual. [17] As has already been mentioned, memory is needed in copying tasks. Other writing tasks require an individual simultaneously to plan and organise his/her thoughts, work out what s/he is going to write, remember how to spell each word, use punctuation and grammar correctly plus construct and join each letter. In examinations, s/he also has to remember what s/he knows about the topic.

As memory plays such an important part in writing tasks (and as memory difficulties are associated with Dyslexia,) the individual may often be diagnosed as having a combination of Graphomotor Dyspraxia and Developmental Dyslexia. In such cases spelling difficulties are also likely to be present *(Developmental Dyslexia - see Book 4)*. As memory difficulties are also found as part of Attention Deficit Disorder and Autistic Spectrum Disorder these conditions can be present too. *(See Book 5.)*

3. Expressive language and concentration difficulties

a) 'Disorganised content often occurs and this is a written extension of associated expressive language problems.' [18] (See Book 4.)

b) *Concentration difficulties* may affect the quality of work.

These difficulties can be caused by various factors; for example, Attention Deficit Disorder will affect concentration (see Book 6). Tiredness and/or stress (which may be caused by having to think of too many things at once) can also cause concentration difficulties. *(This can lead to a vicious circle; tiredness and stress lead to concentration difficulties, leading to tiredness and stress, and so on.)*

Are writing difficulties always associated with the conditions found within the SpLD Profile?

Some writing difficulties, such as an inability to see the text because of short-sightedness, are not associated with the conditions, whilst others might or might not be connected; for example,

1. **Paper position** – All sorts of factors relate to the way that the paper should be positioned for a particular person. If it is not in the right position for the writer it 'can lead to writers adopting such an uncomfortable posture that backache, headache or cramps of all kinds can result'. [19] (However, unusual paper positioning can

The strategies suggested (and tools found within) *Planning and Organisation Solutions* (ISBN 1901544834) and *Creative and Factual Writing Solutions* (ISBN 1901544389) both by Jan Poustie can help when planning and organisation and/or expressive writing difficulties are present.

Sometimes poor writing is not the result of Graphomotor Dyspraxia but of severe Near-vision Dysfunctioning and/or perceptual difficulties, which can cause various difficulties, such as 'glare', out-of-focus writing, and others forms of visual distortion (see Books 1 and 4).

All sorts of factors relate to the way that the paper should be positioned for a particular person.

also indicate that the individual has perceptual and/or visual difficulties. (See Books 1 and 4.)

2. **An awkward or 'floppy posture** can cause backache or visual problems' [20] because the individual is too close to the text etc. but it may also indicate Dyspraxia. (See chapter 1.)

3. **Extremes of height, unusual body proportions or long fingers** may also affect writing skills, since the desk and/or chair may be of incorrect height and the penhold will have to accommodate the fingers. [21]

What are the indicators of Graphomotor Dyspraxia?
Various indicators of Dyspraxia (as mentioned in Chapter 1) will be present, together with many of the following:

1. Preschool indicators

a. Difficulties with hand/eye tasks.

b. Difficulties with general fine motor coordination tasks, such as jigsaws, construction toys, doing up buttons/zips, colouring in (difficulties in staying between the lines), painting/drawing, use of scissors, using eating utensils.

c. Difficulty in controlling the pressure exerted by fingers (a tickle from such children can hurt!)

(Note: some of the difficulties at numbers 1 and 2 above could also be indicators of visual, perceptual and/or concentration difficulties. See Books 1, 4 and 5.)

2. Primary-school indicators
Most of the preschool indicators will still be present at the beginning of primary school. Depending upon the severity of the condition, some, or all, will still be present at the end of primary school. The following indicators are likely to be seen:

a. *Difficulty in doing up shoe laces and/or an inability to consistently do them up sufficiently tightly to ensure that they do not come undone during the day.* The greater the difficulty, the more likely it is that the individual will have to tie their shoe laces frequently during the day, go around with their shoe laces undone, or wear only Velcro or buckle-fastening shoes. (This difficulty may well continue into secondary school, but only those with the most severe difficulties are likely to continue to have this difficulty into adulthood.)

May be able to copy a writing model but may not be able to reproduce it accurately from memory and/or at speed.

Identification Solutions for Coordination Difficulties by Jan Poustie   ISBN 1 901544 87 7

b. *Difficulty in manipulating tools, such as a pen, compass, ruler, saw, comb or toothbrush.* The latter, along with other difficulties that can be seen when Dyspraxia is present, can cause the child to rarely brush his/her hair and/or clean his/her teeth. (Also see Chapter 1.)

c. *Presentation of self.* 'Final touches' to dressing are left undone; for example, shirts/blouses are not tucked in. Both fine- and gross-motor skills are needed for this, so this indicator is common both to those who have Graphomotor Dyspraxia and to those who have another form of Dyspraxia. This can also be an indicator of Autistic Spectrum Disorder – see Book 5.

d. *Presentation of written work.* It takes so much control to just do the writing that the extra effort, concentration and control needed to present work well, such as underlining using a ruler cannot be faced. (If Constructional Dyspraxia is also present, then there might be difficulties for the individual in knowing whether they can fit in a word at the end of a line.) Traditional letter layouts, with the address on the right-hand side of the page, are also likely to be a problem. Poor presentation can also be present in those individuals who have difficulties with writing because of causes other than Graphomotor Dyspraxia (e.g. those who have not been taught the basics well enough and those who are under stress due to spelling difficulties). For both groups, writing is stressful. Good presentation on top of the stress of writing may be an unrealistic expectation until appropriate teaching/provision has been provided and easy and quick strategies for presentation taught.

e. *Inconsistent letter size (of x-height letters) when using lined paper.*

f. *Small writing can be a sign of problems in pen control.* At first glance the writing may look reasonable; however, many of the indicators mentioned in this chapter will be seen when the child is asked to write larger or if the child's writing is enlarged via a photocopier.

g. *Widening of the left-hand margin.*

h. *Pain when writing.* There is evidence that this is unlikely to occur until the age of eleven years. [22] However, changes in the writing demands on students in recent years due to the introduction of SAT's may mean that we are seeing this problem occurring earlier now.

Clothes may appear to have been 'thrown on' rather than 'put on'; e.g. garments may not rest on the shoulders correctly, pocket flaps may be left half in/half out of the pocket. Adults may resort to wearing loose clothes that require few final touches.

i. *Acute turns in connecting joins to letters when it is inappropriate in the writing model being used by the child; for example, a rounded cursive style.*

j. *Absence of joins.*

k. *Irregularities in joins, breaks in the trace of four-to-five-letter words.* By the end of primary school, most children should be able to join each letter of words of this length.

l. *Collisions of letters.*

m. *There is likely to be no change in style once the child no longer has to conform to the school model taught in the early years*

n. *An ability to copy a writing model but not to reproduce it accurately from memory and/or at speed.*

Indicators of Graphomotor Dyspraxia which could also indicate visual difficulties such as long-sightedness or more complex visual and/or perceptual difficulties.
(Also see Books 1 and 4.)

a. *Writing is too large.*

b. *Unsteady writing trace.*

c. *Bad letter or word alignment.*

d. *Insufficient word spacing.*

e. *Incorrect relative height of the various kinds of letters when using lined paper.*

f. *Letter distortion.*

g. *Reversals, inversions of letters and/or confusion as to how to write the letter.* This occurs within groups of letters which if they are inverted and/or reversed, will be the same as another letter; e.g. b/d or q/p is common, i/j is much less so. Some people end up writing such letters as capitals no matter where they occur in the text, because then the confusion cannot occur. This can also be present as part of Dyslexia (Book 4), Autistic Spectrum Disorder (Book 5). When it occurs with numbers, it can be indicative of Dyscalculia (see Mathematics Solutions: an introduction to Dyscalculia).

Indicators of Graphomotor Dyspraxia that could also be the result of any of the above visual and perceptual difficulties and/or spelling difficulties

1. Ambiguous letter forms.
2. Correction of letter forms.

(Also see Book 4.)

Using computers can solve a lot of these student's problems. For apparatus which can help develop keyboard skills see page 49.

Indicators of Graphomotor Dyspraxia that could also be the result of any of the above visual and perceptual difficulties, spelling difficulties and/or expressive language difficulties

1.   Writing slowly.
2.   Only writing a small amount of text.
(Also see Books 4 and 5.)

Various of the above indicators will result in the individual producing poor letter forms that are likely to continue into adulthood

Poor letter forms can result in the individual having spelling difficulties due to the inaccurate remembering of the visual aspect of words. Sometimes, letters are written poorly because the individual is not sure what letter should be written. The same can occur in speech when the individual is not certain as to what sound s/he should be making in the middle of a word and so the sounds are mumbled at this point (see Books 3 and 4 and Verbal/Articulatory Dyspraxia, page 4.)

3. Secondary-school/adulthood indicators
There are likely to be difficulties in many subjects/areas. The higher the intellectual ability of the individual the more likely it is that s/he will have developed strategies to mask his/her difficulties at this stage and so others may be unaware of his/her problems.

A.   *Handwriting indicators*
The following difficulties are likely to be present in secondary school and adulthood:

a.   Presentation of self.

b.   Presentation of written work.

c.   Inconsistent letter size (of x-height letters) when using lined paper.

d.   Acute turns in connecting joins to letters when it is inappropriate in the writing model being used; for example, a rounded cursive style.

e.   Unsteady writing trace.

f.   Reversals, inversions of letters.

g.   Poor letter forms.

There is likely to be no change in style once the student no longer has to conform to the school model taught in the early years.

Secondary-school/adulthood indicators.
Generally, the difficulties may be seen as an uncoordinated use of tools (for example, pen, fork) and/or much slower speed than his/her peer group (of similar intellectual ability) in achieving the task. The individual may also use task avoidance strategies such as misbehaviour.

© Dr Rosemary Sassoon

Callewaert's penhold (reproduced above with the kind permission of Rosemary Sassoon from her book *The Art and Science of Handwriting*, ISBN1871516331) is a much more comfortable grip for some students as it reduces the tension in the hand. In this penhold the writing tool is held between the first and second fingers. (Callewaert was a Belgian neurologist.)

The use of various 'tools' used in school are often a major problem and some students will need 1:1 tuition in such basic apparatus as a ruler and a protractor. Any teacher of a subject which has a practical element (with skills based on the use of any type of tool) may need to devote time to teaching the pupil easy ways to use and control them. Thus the food technology teacher may have to provide specialist tuition in the use of knives, potato peelers and tin openers and the use of special (or different) tools may be necessary in some cases. Potato peelers can be particularly difficult to use and it pays to try out different types of peelers with the student. Peta (UK) Ltd. Tel: 01245 231118) produce a range of scissors and cutting tools which are easy to use. (Also see pages 8 and 41.)

B. *Difficulties that may be seen in other areas*

a. *Fastenings;* for example, open-ended zips (such as those found on anoraks), and shoelaces. If Dressing Dyspraxia is also present, then any activity where changing clothes is required will be stressful; for example, PE and drama (see Chapter 1).

b. *Domestic science;* for example, preparation of food, control of a needle, using a sewing machine.

c. *Science;* for example, control of science equipment. Individuals may exert so much pressure that they break a test tube, and so on.

d. *Design and Technology (DT);* for example, control of the tools, work is likely to be slow and/ or inaccurate. There may be many corrections in drawing. Some individuals may experience difficulties with preparation of food.

e. *Computers;* for example, individuals may have difficulties in controlling the mouse; hold it in non-efficient ways, difficulties in learning to type. Individuals may also dislike using a computer and prefer to use manual writing skills even though such skills may be very weak. (Alternatively, the individual may take to computers like a 'duck to water'.)

f. *Art;* for example, drawing an accurate representation. Individuals are often unhappy with what they produce because they are aware that it does not match what they see and what they feel they should be able to achieve.

g. *All subjects;* for example, drawing of charts, tables and so on.

h. *Geography;* for example, drawing maps and diagrams.

i. *Mathematics;* for example, control of the tools in geometry lessons and in drawing diagrams such as graphs.

Fortunately, many of these difficulties become less important in adulthood, though DIY/sewing and cooking tasks can remain a nightmare. Late development can occur. Much to the author's surprise, she suddenly found that she could draw in her late forties, as both her visual perceptual difficulties and hand control suddenly improved.

Is it easy to spot teenagers and adults who have Graphomotor Dyspraxia via their writing?
No, except in severe cases. This is because writing changes with maturity both in those who have Graphomotor Dyspraxia and in those who are not. Some Dutch research has shown that both groups will increase the size of their writing and omit joins

(in some words and in whole sentences). Also, the letters within words may become so close that letters collide. [23] These changes and deteriorations result in there being less difference in the letter-form quality between those with Graphomotor Dyspraxia and those without it. However, the secondary school indicators seen in section A above can be used to identify the presence of Graphomotor Dyspraxia at this stage.

PART 3 – Referring

One or more of the following referrals may be necessary. Referral to:

1. A doctor; for example, the individual's local GP, school doctor or paediatrician is needed for a more thorough assessment if:

▸ difficulties with the mechanics of writing are noted, and indicators of Graphomotor Dyspraxia are present (as outlined in this chapter); or

▸ mechanical difficulties are noted and there is cause for concern; for example, although it appears that Graphomotor Dyspraxia is not likely, the individual has not responded to appropriate intervention. (The referral is to rule out the possibility of any underlying medical condition and to make further referral to a paediatric occupational therapist (POT) to assess whether Dyspraxia is present. The present shortage of POTs may mean that a long delay occurs before such an assessment can be made [24] and the assessment may never happen at all in the case of older students!

2. A Behavioural Optometrist if Occulomotor Dyspraxia/ Delay is suspected. This type of optometrist conducts a much more thorough assessment than that usually undertaken by the optometrists you find in the High Street. If you want to know whether this sort of difficulty is likely to be present use the PIC 8 checklist in Book 4 and/or find out whether visual distortion difficulties are occurring by using the Poustie Visual Perception Distortion sheets (Appendix 1, *Literacy Solutions* by Jan Poustie et al., ISBN 1 901544 20 6).

3. If both reading and handwriting difficulties are present then parents should make an appointment at their High Street optician to check that the student can see properly - yes, the solution can be as simple as that!

References and footnotes

1. Cato et al. NFER quoted in *Handwriting Helpline*, by Jean Alston

Case study: Jake

In printed writing, letters do not change; for example, each 'a' will look and be written the same, but in in cursive writing an 'a' may be written differently according to which letter is beside it; thus an 'a' joined to a 't' has a different end stroke to an 'a' joined to an 'o'. This can create major problems for those with Graphomotor Dyspraxia. Jake began school in France and so was taught cursive writing from the beginning. He was only able to write very slowly and his joins were poor. He returned to the UK and was provided with a laptop and then went on to gain his doctorate. His case shows what can be achieved if we give our SpLD children the tools they need to succeed!

Further information

Handwriting Interest Group
Felicity Barnes, 6 Fyfield Road,
Ongar, Essex, CM5 0AH
Website: www.
handwritinginterestgroup. org.uk

Recommended Reading
See page 48.

and Jane Taylor (pub. by Dextral Books).

2.   Rosemary Sassoon, *Handwriting: a new perspective* (pub. by Leopard Learning); '40% of girls and 25% of boys reported that they suffered pain when writing.' Also see *The Art and Science of Handwriting*, by Rosemary Sassoon.

3.   *The Art and Science of Handwriting*, by Rosemary Sassoon.

4.   R. Sassoon, *Handwriting: a New Perspective*.

5.   Rosemary Sassoon, *Handwriting: a new perspective*.

6.   *English in the National Curriculum, Jan 1995*. Prepared by the Department for Education (pub. by Her Majesty's Stationery Office, London).

7.   For further information on skills needed for different writing tasks, and for strategies to overcome difficulties contact Next Generation, Taunton.

8.   *Handwriting: a new perspective*, by Rosemary Sassoon.

9.   *Handwriting: a new perspective*, by Rosemary Sassoon.

10.   *Dyslexia and Stress* edited by Tim Miles and Ved Varma (Whurr Publishing)

11.   The *BHK Concise Evaluation Scale for Children's Handwriting* is a test of Dysgraphia (based on the Dutch model of writing) that is used in Holland and Belgium. (Further information on this test is available from: Swets and Zeitlinger, P.O. Box 820, 2160 SZ Lisse, The Netherlands.)

12.   *Encyclopedia of Special Education* edited by Reynolds and Fletcher-Janzen (pub. by Wiley Interscience)

13.   *The Art and Science of Handwriting*, by Rosemary Sassoon

14.   See *Planning and Organisation Solutions* by Jan Poustie.

15.   Rosemary Sassoon: *Handwriting a new perspective*.

16.   See *Literacy Solutions* by Jan Poustie (pub. Next Generation).

17.   See *Planning and Organisation Solutions* by Jan Poustie

18.   Dr Ian McKinlay.

19.   *Handwriting: a new perspective*, by Rosemary Sassoon.

20.   *Handwriting: a new perspective*, by Rosemary Sassoon.

21.   *Handwriting: a new perspective*, by Rosemary Sassoon.

22.   *The Art and Science of Handwriting*, by Rosemary Sassoon.

23.   'Dysgraphic Handwriting Compared with Normal Handwriting' by Dr Lisa Hamstra-Bletz (research psychologist) published in the *Handwriting Review 1994*, pub. By The Handwriting Interest Group (ISBN 1 872832 03 2).

24.   Different health authorities place different priorities on individuals with handwriting difficulties are rooted in Dyspraxia/DCD. In some areas there is provision to assess and treat such individuals (for example, handwriting groups, co-ordination classes and sensory awareness groups) whilst in other areas there may be only limited provision, with long waiting lists.

Conclusion

We know that in order to reach their potential, students who have coordination difficulties need their difficulties to be recognised and supported. Even low-level forms of DCD/DD can have considerable impact upon literacy skills (as shown by Frederick's case study, page 6). In some students only one area of motor functioning is affected but a severe problem in that area can have major impact upon literacy functioning (see Bethany's case study in Book 4). Some students have a very wide range of the SpLD Profile conditions (including DCD/DD) with several at a moderate or severe level. However, even when such a complex profile is present the right intervention can work wonders (see Case study: Child A pages 92 – 95 *Mathematics Solutions: An Introduction to Dyscalculia. Part A*).

As a result of the presence of DCD/DD the individual can be under a great deal of stress. Problems with planning and organisation, with taking longer than others to learn sequences of movements and in controlling the different tools that we meet during our life (e.g. paint brushes for DIY tasks) continue to haunt us throughout adulthood. Individuals will need help and/or support when having to learning to use practical apparatus of any kind and some will require 1:1 tuition in order to achieve competency in such tasks. Such provision will reduce the stress felt by the students and enable them to have the opportunity to reach their potential in adulthood. If this provision is not given, the difficulties (especially with the use of tools), may continue into adulthood with the consequent loss of self-esteem when they may not even be able to put up a shelf or sew on a button that looks either satisfactory and/or does not fall apart. Our stress is made much worse because of a lack of understanding of (and support for) the condition by others. The fact that people may view the presence of our difficulties as being an indication that we are of less intelligence worsens our situation. For most of us who have DCD/DD our biggest problems in an educational setting are:

➤ our weak planning and organisational skills,
➤ problems with learning to use tools of various types at the same speed (and with the same accuracy) as our peers,
➤ the production of large amounts of well presented work at speed by handwritten means (without causing pain and stress to the body).

There is little doubt that the present situation of forcing children with severe co-ordination difficulties to handwrite most of their written work (and in so doing prevent them from showing their

When an individual has many low-level SpLDs it is easy to underestimate his/her potential. Individuals who have DCD/DD can succeed in school and in the workplace (and can go on academically to further and higher education). However, such students will need encouragement, support and plenty of reinforcement when doing tasks they find difficult. This can be achieved if the student's range of difficulties (including any associated Specific Learning Difficulties) is identified and acted upon. All the professionals involved need to work as a team in partnership with the individual and his/her parents/spouse.

Within the supportive teaching environment our students also need their behaviour to be understood and gradually modified as appropriate. Of equal importance is that students should understand the cause of their difficulties and be made aware of their skills. Students should be enabled to shine in at least one area (leisure or academic) so that the low self-esteem that can spoil their lives is reduced. (The depression that can exist alongside low self-esteem can be so destructive that the student attempts suicide.)

knowledge base) is educationally unsound. It is a little like forcing someone with a broken leg to walk one mile every day. Such a practice would be regarded as inhuman. No adult would expect such treatment and neither should our children. Our educational system needs to recognise that the world of the computer and superior word-processing programs has arrived. Already many of us in the workplace rarely use handwriting except for a hastily scribbled note, a shopping list or to sign a credit card voucher, addressing envelopes and note-taking. For many of us the main form of leisure writing now is text messaging and the typing of e-mails or messages in an internet chat room.

However, using technology is not without problems of its own as it too can cause problems in the way that our hand and body function. Much greater demands are being placed on us to record, write and use the hand in very repetitive movements than ever before. As adults we have to reply to the often huge quantities of e-mails received daily in the workplace. The younger members of our population have fast become bewitched by computer games and text messaging which can put a huge amount of strain on the thumb and first finger tendons and joints. Computers and keypads are commonplace everywhere (even in the supermarket).

All types of workplaces require that their employees become computer literate, which has stimulated a huge upsurge in courses such as Computer Literacy and Information Technology (CLAIT). In our desire to provide IT skills for all, many are missing the essentials of IT training; e.g. how to do all of these tasks without putting undue stress on the human hand and frame. Some teachers may teach the student good keyboarding technique but many other teachers will know little about it. There may be little instruction on how to sit and hold the hands and arms to avoid repetitive strain injury (RSI) or little knowledge of the ergonomics of computing; e.g. the correct height of the chair, the table, the VDU screen plus the necessary body posture to avoid back and muscle strain. Keyboarding (typing) is a motor function which we learn by putting the correct sequence of movements into our motor memory. Once learnt incorrectly it is very difficult to retrain the student. Therefore, such skills need to be trained in primary school before our children develop bad habits. Some teachers seem to have a misinformed desire to always ensure that the student only ever sees lower case letters. So, they replace the normal uppercase keyboard with one which only has lower case letters (e.g. through a new keyboard or using stickers). What is not realised is that only one pair of letters can be confused for each other in upper case (M and W) whereas in lower case we have many letters to confuse; e.g. j/l, h/y, b/d/q/p. The use of a lower case keyboard will only make it more difficult for our students who have Dyslexia or Occulomotor Dyspraxia. Society is making the transition to word-processing as the dominant method of recording at a rapid rate but our educational system is not. Primary school children's bodies are pliable. So, the pain that results from their lack of training at this age shows up later when the pressure of recording increases; e.g. at GCSE and A level. By this time they will be under almost intolerable pressure (and in considerable pain) when trying to achieve the speed necessary to produce the necessary written output.

Within our schools we still have a system where handwritten notes are the norm and where handwritten recording is expected for the majority of written work. Students with co-ordination and/or reading difficulties need to be provided with pre-written notes. However, that results in high photocopying bills that schools may not wish to meet. (It also requires all lessons to be prepared well in advance by all of their teachers.) Some of our teachers may feel that meeting the needs of our students with DCD/DD is just one thing too many. Most teachers are already stressed by their workload and many feel extremely threatened by the government's need for almost continuous change and the government's desire that they will read the equivalent of an Amazonian rainforest's quantity of paper per week. Teachers are under so much pressure that some may feel that meeting the need's of their students who have Dyspraxia is the final straw that breaks the camel's back. In the workplace, clerical staff are provided with a computer station on their desk – few schools provide the same facility for our teachers and teaching assistants. We now have a situation where our educators may well feel threatened when a student brings a laptop into the classroom for fear that they will be asked to help sort out any problems that the student may experience when using the equipment.

Even certain GCSE courses that were once regarded as 'practical subjects' demand vast quantities of written output on the part of our students. Thus we have courses such as food technology which demand that all work be presented in A3 format (a paper size which most printers cannot print onto) thus causing much of the work to be done by hand. A further complication may arise if the home PC system is incompatible with the system at school and so work started at school has to be re-typed at home.
There is a need to help those with handwriting difficulties to reach their potential and so enrich our society. The needs of our

Educators need to be aware that furniture will affect handwriting and that both the student who has outgrown his/her desk and the one for whom it is too large are disadvantaged when it comes to handwriting. The trend in the UK to use tables (instead of angled desks) and to arrange student's seating so that they have to move into uncomfortable positions in order to copy from the black/ whiteboard can also make it much more difficult for the student. Yes, it is very difficult sometimes to ensure that students have the appropriate furniture and are best placed to see the board but, especially for those with coordination difficulties, the effort must be made.

Identification Solutions for Coordination Difficulties by Jan Poustie   ISBN 1 901544 87 7

Those students who do not have computers at home are disadvantaged from producing much of their other assignment work on computer. There is anecdotal evidence of some teachers awarding a higher grade to computer-generated work than to handwritten work because the former is easier for the teacher to read and the presentation is so much more superior. This can result in a 'halo effect', where handwritten work from disadvantaged students may be perceived as being of a lesser quality than the computer-generated work of some their peers. A token lesson on computers at school does not provide the much needed IT experience that these students need.

students can be met if there is adequate training of our teachers and workplace trainers. Such training has to cover not only the recognition of, and provision for, those with handwriting difficulties but also appropriate alternative strategies to writing. The use of computers for all writing intensive tasks is common practice in many workplaces. Such practice cannot occur in our educational establishments until our educators are enabled to feel confident in the use of their hardware and software (and their hardware and software resources are brought up-to-date). It also cannot occur unless those educators are adequately supported and trained in ICT skills. Some educators do not even know how to restart a computer after it has crashed (e.g. by pressing its reset button or the Ctrl, Alt and Del keys simultaneously). As a result computers can be left idle for several days until the ICT specialist has the time to get to the machine. The situation in many schools (especially primary ones) is made worse because the teacher who is given the responsibility for ICT is also likely to have a full teaching load. S/he therefore cannot leave his/her class to sort out the technical problem which is stopping the computer from working.

Everyone still demands 'good quality handwriting' as they think that it is being written for the benefit of the reader alone, whereas the crucial writing skill our students need to develop by A level is the ability to record information quickly. (This may result in a barely legible scribble but it serves its purpose.) We are damaging our students, we are stressing those that teach them. After all, whatever our students write our teachers have to mark! We have become a society that expects paperwork to come in reams from everybody as proof that teaching has occurred. This ridiculous situation is continuously being fuelled by yet more demands by the government and an inspection system that teachers feel must be fed by student's written output. We have to change our attitude towards handwriting. Our examining boards and our government have to reduce the amount of written work that is expected of our students. In a world where output is everything, there is little time for even the most dedicated teacher to devote to the actual mechanics of teaching handwriting. The introduction of the national curriculum has brought with it a shift in focus from the student to the curriculum. Unless we change this situation our students (and their educators) will continue to suffer in our educational establishments.

Society's high demand for written output is becoming a strain on all of us involved in education but for those with writing difficulties it is much worse. Their difficulties can place them at a severe disadvantage. The 'problem' may lie in **their** hands - but the solution to it is in **ours!**

Identification Solutions for Coordination Difficulties by Jan Poustie   ISBN 1 901544 87 7

APPENDIX I
Assessments
For convenience, the parent is referred to as 'her' and the student as 'he' in this section.

Dyspraxia/DCD Assessment
A "multidisciplinary assessment" will include a variety of the following assessments all of which may also take place separately at different stages of the individual's life. Each specialist uses different assessment tools; e.g. clinical observation of the individual, the use of checklists and standardised assessments.

Assessments for Dyspraxia/DCD
Either the school or the parents can ask the school doctor/GP to refer the child for Dyspraxia/DCD. S/he may refer the child to a paediatrician or directly to *paediatric physio/occupational therapists* for an assessment of fine and gross motor (including Graphomotor Dyspraxia and other writing difficulties) sensory and cognitive (thinking) skills. (See pages 17-19.)

The paediatric occupational therapist will, as part of a holistic assessment, assess a variety of cognitive, motor, language and sensory (e.g. visual) skills. There are a variety of assessment tools which the therapist can use among them are the *Movement ABC* by Henderson and Sugden and the *Bruininks-Oseretsky Test of Motor Proficiency*. They both contain sub-tests which involve the individual carrying out a variety of fine motor activities which can be used to measure the foundation skills of fine motor speed and dexterity which are necessary for handwriting. For full details of assessment see Table 4, page 19.

Assessment may include the use of various standardised tests and/or the use of checklists either available nationally or developed by individual centres. As *speech and language difficulties* are commonly associated with Dyspraxia/DCD an assessment for this is usually recommended. This can be made by either the parent or the school making a referral to her local NHS hospital's Speech and Language unit for a language assessment on her behalf or make a direct referral to the unit herself by telephoning/writing to the unit and asking for a referral form. Such assessments are free under the national health. *Vision* should always be checked but near-vision dysfunction is so specialised a field that even non-behavioural optometrists/school nurses with an interest in this field may miss the signs of visual delay/Occulomotor Dyspraxia. (See Book 4.) Doctors will make referrals to orthoptists (based in

hospitals) and/or optometrists to assess different areas of visual function. *At present Behavioural optometrists are only available privately (see Book 4 for contacts).*

Assessments for medical conditions that can be seen alongside Dyspraxia/DCD
Various professionals may assess the individual at various stages of his life. The child with severe/moderate Dyspraxia/DCD is likely to receive assessments at an earlier age and from a wider variety of professionals. Any of the following: Health Visitors, School doctors/nurses, GP's, community paediatricians and child and adolescent psychiatrists are likely to be involved in the referral and assessment process of the moderate/severe child.

Various medical professionals may be involved in assessing one or more of a range of medical conditions, which are associated with dyspraxia (see page 11). If signs are found which could indicate a neurological disease of a specific nature then the child may also be referred to one of the few paediatric neurologists in the UK. An educational psychologist may assess for Moderate Learning Difficulties (which can occur alongside Dyspraxia/DCD) and/or for behavioural difficulties. The latter may also be assessed by a paediatrician or child and adolescent psychiatrist.

Educational assessments
We have some tests that can be used by educators; for example, *Movement Assessment Battery for Children*, by Henderson and Sugden (pub. by The Psychological Corporation Ltd., London). This is a very expensive assessment tool but the Checklist can be bought separately. Also available is the Portwood Motor Screening Test (found in *Developmental Dyspraxia* by Madeleine Portwood).

Specific Learning Difficulty in literacy
If the individual has difficulties in learning to read and/or spell then a literacy assessment may be necessary (see Book 4).

Mathematical assessment
A specific learning difficulty in numeracy/mathematics (Dyscalculia) is common amongst those who have Dyspraxia so a mathematical assessment should be carried out if the parent/teacher has concerns in this

area (see *Mathematics Solutions - An Introduction to Dyscalculia Parts A and B* by Jan Poustie published by Next Generation).

Educationalists/educational psychologist assessment
These specialist assess intellectual function (though at present only educational psychologists can assess for intellectual functioning using the WISC and BAS tests). In order to obtain such assessments contact your local school, Local Educational Authority's Psychological service or Special Educational Needs Support Team. You can also find a private specialist with a special interest in this field by contacting your specialist agency coordinator; e.g. local Dyspraxia Foundation co-ordinator and local dyslexia support group. The British Dyslexia Association has lists of accredited teachers. (See page iv for contacts.)

Assessing writing difficulties
Various aspects of writing can be assessed using a variety of assessment tools including observation, standardised/non-standardised tests and checklists. A comprehensive assessment by teachers and educational psychologists would include the following:
A. Error rate
B. Spelling: The more errors made, the more time that will be needed to be spent on corrections. Whilst many primary school pupils can cope with having to do three or four corrections for each page of work, most will find it a loss to self-esteem and time-consuming if more than double than that are needed on a regular basis. This is likely to result in them using only the words they can spell and so masking their true intellectual ability.
C. Overall errors: *(e.g. grammar, spelling, punctuation)* - Most individuals will be able to cope with correcting up to 5% of their work
    (1 error in every 20 words). Many will find having to correct much more than that (on a regular basis) so daunting that they are unlikely to be motivated to write in any quantity as the number of corrections that they will have to make is just too great.
D Posture and pen hold
E Letter forms, their construction, spacing and alignment etc.
Writing speed may also be assessed. The complexity and variety of writing tasks has caused there to be debate amongst professionals regarding the validity of such an assessment. There is also debate as to what

task should be used as the basis of assessment and how long the task should take. [1]

The PATOSS organisation (www.patoss-dyslexia.org, Tel: 01386 712650) has conducted some research into writing speeds. They have also published the book *Providing for candidates with special assessment needs during GCE (A-Level), VCE, GCSE & GNVQ* by Gill Backhouse (ISBN 0953931501). This book provides information on determining writing speed and tests that can be used for assessing handwriting. There appears to be a wide range of 'average' writing rates. This is of great concern because it would appear that many of our GCSE courses and other public examinations have an unrealistic expectation of writing speed of their students. (This results in students gaining lower grades because they are not able to write enough information in exams and being put under undue pressure for assignment work. The pressure put on the student to write faster can then result in conditions such as repetitive strain injury.)

Research (by Allcock, 2000 and Waine, 2000) reported in Backhouse's book indicates that the average writing speed for Year 10/11 pupils when doing free writing tasks is 15 wpm. Free writing tasks involve the student writing an essay about something that they know; e.g. their favourite film. Such tasks are less demanding than examination questions; e.g. history questions which require not only that the student can write his/her ideas in an understandable fashion but also that s/he accesses from memory facts relating to the question. It would seem likely that writing speed is one of the factors that determine the grade the student receives at GCSE. We need more research into this area. It would be useful, for instance, for us to know the average writing speed in the top GCSE sets compared with the bottom GCSE sets.

The use of the indicators found in the various chapters of this book plus appropriate assessment tools will enable the assessor to make the necessary referrals to other specialists as appropriate; e.g.
1. The use of the indicators in Books 1 and 4 (on how to recognise visual and perceptual difficulties) will help to determine whether there is also a visual and/or perceptual aspect to the difficulty. The reader will then know whether referral to a optometrist, orthoptist, behavioural optometrist and/or a specialist in Scotopic Sensitivity Irlen Syndrome is needed. [2]

2. The *Aston Index* sub-test 11 (pub. LDA, Tel: 01945 463441) plus the use of the indicators in PICs 1 and 6 (Book 2) and in Books 3 and 5 will determine whether a referral to a speech and language therapist for an assessment of expressive language is needed and/or a referral to a doctor for further referral for Autistic Spectrum Disorder is needed. (Miscue analysis could be used here i.e. looking at the types of errors made such as use of prepositions, difficulties in expressing abstract concepts, grammar, word meanings and syntax.)

3. Attention deficits can be noted during assessment and these observations plus the use of the indicators in PIC 5 (Book 2) and in Books 1 and 5 will help the assessor determine whether a referral to a specialist such as a paediatric neurologist/educational psychiatrist is necessary.

4. Any of the following may be used to determine whether difficulties with the mechanics of handwriting are causing problems. Those that give advice based on the teacher/therapist observing examples of handwriting are: *Helping with Handwriting* by Rosemary Sassoon, *Handwriting Checklist* by Alston and Taylor, *The diagnosis and Remediation of Handwriting Difficulties* by Stott, Moyes and Henderson and *Handwriting Helpline* [3] by Alston and Taylor. These tools also provide background information on writing and remediation strategies with the information differing according to the background of the writers. Alternatively, an assessor can use the fine motor co-ordination tasks and observation of handwriting sub-tests which are part of the *Aston* Index; e.g. sub-tests 3, 4, 10, 11 and 17. [4]

Referral to a doctor; e.g. the individual's local GP, school doctor or paediatrician is needed for a more thorough assessment if:

1. Difficulties with the mechanics of writing are noted plus indicators of Graphomotor Dyspraxia are present (as outlined in Chapter 2) or

2. Mechanical difficulties are noted and there is cause for concern; e.g. although it appears that Graphomotor Dyspraxia is not likely the individual has not responded to appropriate intervention.

(Such referrals are important to rule out the possibility of any underlying medical condition and to make further referral to a paediatric occupational therapist to assess whether Dyspraxia/DCD is present.) The present shortage of such paediatric occupational therapists may mean a long delay before such an assessment can be made [5] or that in the case of the older student such an assessment is never made.

Further information

For information on how to refer to specialists see page 22.

References and footnotes

1. For further information on this see:
   ▸ *Literacy Solutions* by Jan Poustie
   ▸ *Writing output and writing speeds* by Jean Alston published in 'Dyslexia Review' - *The Journal of the Dyslexia Institute Guild Vol. 6, No. 2, Autumn 1994* (pub. by The Dyslexia Institute.)
   ▸ *The Art and Science of Handwriting* by Rosemary Sassoon

2. A doctor (local GP etc.) can refer you to an optometrist (either at an NHS hospital) or one of the many who do both private and NHS work in any town. He can also refer you to an orthoptist (available in your local NHS hospital). There are very few behavioural optometrists in the UK. See Book 4 for the relevant address.

3. This was originally designed as an 'experimental instrument' and so its scoring system is not as easy to use as those of some other assessment tools and the reliability levels for it are very modest. (Its authors regard it as a training resource; both in initial teacher education and for use by those who are involved in helping individuals overcome writing difficulties.)

4. If assessing a student for external examination purposes then see *Providing for candidates with special assessment needs during GCE (A-Level), VCE, GCSE & GNVQ* by Gill Backhouse, pub. PATOSS.

5. Different health authorities place different priorities on individuals whose handwriting difficulties are based in Dyspraxia/DCD and the problems that this causes. In some areas there is provision to assess and treat such individuals; e.g. handwriting groups, co-ordination classes and sensory awareness groups whilst in other areas there may be only limited provision with long waiting lists.

If Graphomotor Dyspraxia or other difficulties with the mechanics of writing (e.g. letter construction) are found, what can the teacher/ parent do to help the individual overcome the difficulties?

Difficulties not associated with Graphomotor Dyspraxia. Some difficulties such as cramped writing/poor layout may be due to the individual still obeying an instruction that is long out-of-date; e.g. being told in primary school to fit more onto a page so as to use less paper. The identification and solving of this sort of difficulty plus teaching strategies to overcome difficulties in the mechanics of writing may require some 1:1 tuition. For this group and (especially for those who also have literacy difficulties) Alston and Taylor's *Handwriting Helpline* may be suitable as some of the strategies within it integrate literacy and writing skills. Some of the information from Sassoon's *Helping with Handwriting*; e.g. pen holds, strategies for overcoming pain, left-handedness and tips on achieving faster writing etc. are also likely to be needed.

Notes:

1. Research has shown that alternative pen holds can be faster than the 'dynamic tripod', which is commonly used in UK schools. See *An analysis of children's pen holds* by Sassoon, Nimmo-Smith and Wing in *Graphonomics: Contemporary Research in Handwriting*, H S R Kao, G P van Galen, R Hoosain (eds) pub. B V (North Holland), 1986.
2. some writing difficulties can occur because the student does not understand the mechanics of the writing tool that s/he is using. Thus one student thought that if he pressed hard then his fountain pen would work better.

Difficulties due to Graphomotor Dyspraxia
Individuals who have Dyspraxia/DCD are likely to have difficulties in learning new motor based skills/movements. Although they may appear to have learnt them in a teaching session they are often unable to transfer this knowledge to the classroom/workplace. So, for this group strategies based against a writing model that is not their own are unlikely to work. Sassoon's *Helping with Handwriting* is useful here as it provides details about how to adjust the individual's own handwriting.

The information on pen hold (especially alternative pen holds that can reduce pain for some individuals; e.g. Callewaert's (see page 37), hand position etc. is also likely to be essential if the teacher is to provide effective help.

If Graphomotor Dyspraxia is suspected what can be done if a paediatric occupational therapist's assessment is either unavailable or delayed?

There are various books, which give the details of simple and fun exercises that are a starting point in dealing with many of the underlying difficulties that are found as part of Dyspraxia/DCD; e.g. *Watch me I can do it* by Neralie Cocks (pub. Simon & Schuster.) These activities require very little in the way of equipment. If you are not sure which ones to do, a 'rule of thumb' method would be to try each of the tasks that are recommended (for the appropriate age group). Only practise those activities which the individual does not find very easy. If a task is particularly difficult only expect the individual to do it initially for a very short time (for some this may only be one or two minutes or less) until they have built up some skill in the activity. It is exceptionally important that our educators and parents take note of the following advice from Rosemary Sassoon:

> Handwriting exercises are torture and even when not productive they still have to carry on with handwriting exercises. Such exercises may make the person's fine motor movements more accurate eventually but at what cost? In order to achieve a result the child has to face the daily drudgery and the negative feedback of their own written trace.

Workbooks are not the solution to our student's problems. A much kinder way is to play games to encourage fine motor skill development; e.g. *Tiddly Winks* (*Leaping Frogs* from the Early Learning Centre) and *Pick Up sticks*. A large range of very useful games are available from the Happy Puzzle Company (www.happypuzzle.co.uk/ or telephone 0800 376 3727). Professionals need to be aware of the fatigue and the stress of students when they are re-educating their muscles and that this is very tiring for them. The person who can write acceptably but slowly may never be able to speed up to meet the needs of the teacher and the educational setting. Tension is reflected back to the pupil in his/her handwriting, so the child's misery is compounded when s/he sees his/her poor handwriting - no-one needs to comment upon it as the s/he is only too aware of his/her problems. The educator needs to find something to praise rather than criticise something which the student cannot control. There is always something which is better than the rest of the page; e.g. a particular join, a single word.

Handwriting

Handwriting review (pub. yearly by the Handwriting Interest Group)

Handwriting Helpline by Alston & Taylor (pub. Dextral books)

Skipping not Tripping by Neralie Cocks (pub. Simon & Schuster)

Praxis makes Perfect (pub. The Dyspraxia Foundation)

Handwriting - a new perspective by Rosemary Sassoon (pub. Leopard Learning)

Helping with handwriting by Rosemary Sassoon (pub. John Murray)

The Art and Science of Handwriting by Rosemary Sassoon (pub. Intellect).

Which Handwriting Scheme by the Handwriting Interest Group (www.handwritinginterestgroup.org.uk). Details the different schemes which are available.

Literacy Solutions and *Planning and Organisation Solutions* both by Jan Poustie (pub. Next Generation)

Apparatus/books which may be useful

Write from the start by Ion Teoderescu and Lois Addy (Tel: 01945 463441) writing scheme.

Write Angle (supplier Philip & Tacey Ltd, Tel: 01264 332171). This slanting writing desk creates the right angle for easier writing.

StartWrite computer program (Tel: 01666 843200) enables you to make your own handwriting worksheets based on your own text. Arrows show the direction of the first stroke of each letter. Exit strokes are shown for each letter. Those with severe problems will need adult help so that they know the next directions that they have to move in when creating letters and how to create the joining strokes between letters.

Keyboard Crazy (Tel: 0151 226 5000) can be used to teach keyboard skills to pre-school and primary children without them needing access to a computer. It has a backing board, one side of which has pictures to go with each of the letters; e.g. a picture of zebra for 'z'. The pictures can help the child to learn the sounds that the letters make plus learn the keys' locations. It also has lower case and upper case plastic key inserts. Only use the lower case inserts when matching keys with the lowercase backing board which has pictures.

Students who have Dyslexia and/or visual difficulties
These students may find the above matching activity easier to play if they use *Wikki Stix* (Tel: 01494 538999) to create 3D letters on the lower case key inserts. Then they can feel their way around the letters - this makes letter confusion less likely. For the rest of the games avoid using the lower case backing board which does not have pictures and the lower case key inserts *Wikki Stix* can be bought as sets of sticks or as part of packs; e.g. the dinosaurs in the *Fun Activity Set* to create all sorts of pictures.

Developmental Dyspraxia/ Developmental Coordination Disorder

Midline (magazine published by the Dyspraxia Foundation and available from them, see page iv for contact details).

Watch Me, I Can Do It! by Neralie Cocks (pub. by Simon & Schuster). The first edition of this book was originally published under the title of *Skipping, not Tripping*.

Praxis Makes Perfect II, edited by Penny Hunt (published by The Dyspraxia Foundation, ISBN 0 9534344 0).

Take Time, by Mary Nash-Wortham and Jean Hunt (pub. Robinswood Press).

Developmental Dyspraxia - a Practical Manual for Parents and Professionals by Madeleine Portwood (pub. by David Fulton Publishers, ISBN 85346 573 9).

Developmental Motor Speech Disorders by M. Crary (pub. by Whurr Publishers Ltd.)

Dyspraxia - A Handbook for Therapists by Michèle Lee and Jenny French, (Association of Paediatric Chartered Physiotherapists), available from Carol Foster MCSP, Superintendent Physiotherapist, The Children's Hospital, Middleway, Birmingham.

Graded Activities for Children with Motor Difficulties by James P. Russell (pub. Cambridge University Press).

Perceptuo-motor difficulties (Theory and strategies to help children, adolescents and adults) by Dorothy E Penso (Pub. Chapman and Hall).

Literacy Solutions, Mathematics Solutions – An Introduction to Dyscalculia Parts A and B and *Planning and Organisation Solutions* all by Jan Poustie (pub. by Next Generation) provide information on further titles (and strategies) that will be of use.

Appendix 4: Developmental Dyspraxia/DCD
Teaching Guidance

Teacher/parent partnership

Having empathy with the student and his/her difficulties is important but by itself it will not be enough to enable the student to overcome the difficulties. It is essential that the teacher accepts and recognises the student's difficulties. The educator also needs to:

1. Make use of the advice in the reports made by the various professionals; e.g. a paediatric occupational therapist and a paediatric physiotherapist reports.

2. Use multisensory teaching techniques, where the senses of movement, vision, speech and hearing are used simultaneously. If they are not used simultaneously then the teaching method is not multisensory and so will be less effective. (The senses of touch and smell can also be used if wished.) Note single sensory techniques will need to be used when Central/Auditory Processing Disorder is present.

3. Be prepared to adapt your teaching technique to the pupil's needs (including using the appropriate learning style; e.g. qualitative, or, quantitative styles) and modifying PE activities so that the student who has Dyspraxia/DCD is enabled to participate. See *Planning and Organisation Solutions* by Jan Poustie (published by Next Generation) and *Accelerated Learning in the Classroom* by Alistair Smith (published by Network Educational Press Ltd.) for further information on Learning Styles.

4. If there is a SpLD in numeracy and/or literacy (e.g. Dyscalculia/Dyslexia) some tuition in a 1:1 environment is likely to be necessary for the child to achieve his/her potential. See *Mathematics Solutions - An Introduction to Dyscalculia Parts A and B* and *Literacy Solutions* both by Jan Poustie (published by Next Generation).

5. Accept that the student's fidgeting, clumsiness and over-reaction to certain situations are not within his/her control.

6. Be aware that the student may be under stress throughout the whole school day although s/he does not appear to be so and that this occurs even when s/he has very good relationship with his/her educators. This can be caused by the student fearing that s/he will make errors, be clumsy or that s/he will be told off by his/her educator (or, if in a group lesson that s/he will be teased by his/her peer group.)

7. Follow Michèle Lee's advice:
"Seat the child appropriately in the classroom, i.e. not near a window/door or at the back of the classroom where s/he can become easily distracted or not hear the instructor or see the blackboard easily."

8. Teach strategies that will help individuals to overcome difficulties in short term memory, organisational and planning skills.

9. Teachers of a subject which has a practical element (with skills based on the use of any type of tool) will need to be prepared to devote time to teaching the pupil easy ways to use and control the tool(s).

10. Teach the presentation skills that are needed for your subject; e.g. drawing charts, underlining using a ruler and presenting maths work neatly.

11. Provide support for students who need to use a computer during your lesson (including strategies to avoid the student being teased by his/her peer group when using the equipment).

12. Provide tuition (1:1 may be necessary) in the use of practical apparatus.

13. Enable your student to use alternative writing tools and penholds to see if that makes it easier for him/her to write.

14. If handwriting difficulties are present then enable the student to use alternative means of recording work; e.g. computers, audio tapes, Mind Maps.

15. Be proactive in stopping the bullying of your DCD/DD students (including verbal teasing).

APPENDIX 5
Poustie Identification Checklists
PICS 4 and 10

These checklists are designed to provide a starting point for those who need to be able to identify the SpLD Profile conditions (e.g. educators, parents and students) so that appropriate provision and referrals for diagnosis to specialist professionals can occur. Principally designed for school age children and adults each checklist explains which items should be used for which students. Primary and secondary children: use all the list. Adults: use items marked # unless told otherwise in the instructions on the checklist. Pre-school (3 - 4 years): use only the shaded items (also see right-hand column below).

Method of use for each of the PIC checklists:

1. Fill in the checklist. Note: each statement has a rating scale (the numbers in the right-hand column) which ranges from 1-5 .
   5= this happens a lot; 1= this happens rarely. Enter the behaviours/ indicators which are present by ticking the appropriate boxes in each checklist. Only tick those behaviours that are present. Circle each of the elements in each question that are present; e.g. in question A8 of PIC 4 (on page 52) if difficulties have been noted in 'people being too close to them' and 'dislike of tight clothes' then both these phrases should be circled. Parents may now choose to hand in the checklist to the SENCO/AENCO of their child's school or to their GP.

2. Professionals (and interested parents) should follow the advice at the bottom of the relevant checklists as to which of the book/s in the library should now be read. Thus ticking question B5 on PIC 4 advises you to read Books 3 and 6 of the *Identification Solutions for Specific Learning Difficulties Library*. Each of the books in this library contain additional checklists and a wider range of indicators (including more detailed information of the indicators seen in pre-school children and adults). The books contain instructions for making referrals to the correct medical/ educational professionals.

3. Enter the score in the 'results' box. Circle yes or no as appropriate in the 'Results' and 'Is a referral advised' boxes. Always include a copy of the relevant PIC when making a referral.

4. If the student scores positively on the PIC checklist/s and his/her profile matches the information within the relevant books from this library it does not automatically mean that the student has the condition/s. However, there are indications that the condition/s may be present and so a referral for a diagnostic assessment via the student's GP is recommended. If the majority of the statements on a checklist are ticked, then there is a strong possibility that the condition is present. In such cases it is always advised that provision, within an educational and home setting, should be put in to place for the likely condition whilst awaiting for such an assessment to take place. (Note: the individual should be referred to an educational psychologist, the Learning Support Department of the educational establishment or to a SpLD specialist if Dyslexia or Dyscalculia are thought to be present.)

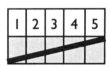

If a behaviour/indicator is not present
Put a long diagonal line through the complete right-hand column; i.e. one line through all the boxes 1 – 5 if the behaviour/indicator is not present.

Assessing 3 –5 year old
The reader is advised to refer to *From birth to five years: children's developmental progress* by Mary D Sheridan (ISBN 0415164583, pub. Routledge), along with using the PIC checklists when making an identification of a child aged 3 –5 years. It is an excellent and easy-to-understand book. It provides information on the developmental stages of children. It covers social behaviour, play, vision, fine movements, hearing, speech, posture and large movements. Also see pages 19-32 *Developmental Dyspraxia* by Madeleine Portwood.

PIC 4: Poustie Identification Checklist for
Developmental Dyspraxia/DCD/Motor Coordination Difficulties (3 years to adult)

GENERAL INFORMATION								
Assessor:			Method of Assessment:					
Name of student	Date of Consultation		Student's age		Date of birth			
Results: Number of items scoring between 2 and 6 points = Does the student's profile fit the information in Book 6? Yes/No					Is a referral advised: Yes/No			

Each statement has a rating scale: 5= this happens a lot, 1= this happens rarely. Only tick those behaviours that are present.

All items may be seen in school age children. Shaded areas = may be seen from 3 years, # = carries on into adulthood.		1	2	3	4	5
A1	Poor balancing skills; e.g. may have difficulties in learning to roller blade, to ride a tricycle/bike. #					
A2	Difficulties in remembering and carrying out motor-based tasks. #					
A3	Difficulties relating to spatial awareness and judging distances; e.g. may have problems with catching a ball, may put mugs too close to the edge of a table, may knock into things. #					
A4	Lack of coordination between the two sides of the body; e.g. may find it difficult to learn to play musical instruments and to swim. #					
A5	Poor planning and organisational skills or emotional immaturity as compared with peer group. May become easily distressed. #					
A6	Clumsiness; e.g. may press too hard and break things, knock into people and objects. #					
A7	Poor presentation of work/self. May look untidy and work may be untidy. #					
A8	Sensory hypo/hypersensitivity. Any of the following may be present: may actively dislike certain noises, textures of cloth, textures in the mouth, sensations (e.g. dislike of having hair cut, teeth cleaned), people being too close to them (including a dislike of crowds) or tight clothes. #					
A9	Fidgeting, restlessness. (May prefer to lie down rather than sit when doing homework.) #					
B1	Difficulties in finding things against a busy background; e.g. difficulties in finding an item on a notice board or in a drawer with any ease. #					
B2	Poor and/or slow handwriting. #					
B3	Difficulties in doing tasks which need good control over fingers (fine motor control) or spatial skills; e.g. dressing, tying shoelaces, writing, drawing, using cutlery. #					
B4	Difficulties in reading, writing or spelling. #					
B5	Sucking, swallowing, and chewing difficulties; difficulties in learning to blow his/her nose; speech and/or language difficulties. #					
B6	Difficulties in mathematics, dislike playing games that use numbers or spatial skills. #					
B7	Difficulties in carrying out a sequence of actions; e.g. the correct sequence for threading a sewing machine, doing up buttons, putting on a coat. #					

Scoring: If the rating is 2-5 for two or more of the items in section A or B (Pre-school, School age and adult students) read Book 6, if the student's profile fits then refer (also read Book 1).
If the rating is 2-5 for: ,
▸ **A9:** read Books 1, 5 and 6,

▸ **B2 or B3:** read Books 4 and 6,
▸ **B4:** read Books 1, 3 and 4,
▸ **B5:** read Books 3 and 6,
▸ **B6:** read *Mathematics Solutions Part A by Jan Poustie et al* ISBN 1 901544 45 1.

PIC 10: Poustie Identification Checklist for Graphomotor Dyspraxia (6 years to adult)

GENERAL INFORMATION

Assessor:	Method of assessment:		
Name of student	Date of consultation	Student age	Date of birth

Results: Number of items scoring between 2 and 6 points =
Does the student's profile fit the information in Book 6? Yes/No

Is a referral advised: Yes/No

Each statement has a rating scale: 5= this happens a lot, 1= this happens rarely. Only tick those behaviours that are present.

All items may be seen in school age children and in adults.		1	2	3	4	5
A	Student makes errors when constructing letters when writing.					
B	Widening of the left-hand margin. *					
C	Able to copy a writing model but not be able to reproduce it accurately from memory and/or at speed. *					
D	Inconsistent letter size (of x-height letters) when using lined paper. *					
E	Collision of letters. *					
F	Very small or very large writing.					
G	Little, or no change in style once the student no longer has to conform to the school model taught in the early years.					
H	Slow handwriting.					
I	Unsteady writing trace; e.g. the writing does not flow smoothly, looks untidy. *					
J	Bad letter or word alignment.					
K	Insufficient word spacing. *					
L	Acute turns in connecting joins to letters when it is inappropriate in the writing model being used by the student; e.g. a rounded cursive style.					
M	Incorrect relative height of the various kinds of letters such as those that have parts of the letter going below the line (e.g. the tails of y, j) or to the top of the writing line (e.g. h, l) when using lined paper. *					
N	Letter distortion. *					
O	Reversals, inversions of letters and/or confusion as to how to write the letter.					
P	Absence of joins (only relevant if the student has been taught to join letters a year or more ago.)					
Q	Ambiguous letter forms; e.g. the reader is not sure which letter has been written. *					
R	Finds it painful to write (usually only present from about eleven years onwards). *					
	Other Skills					
1	Difficulties in manipulating tools; e.g. pen, compass, ruler, saw, comb and toothbrush (these difficulties may have reduced by adulthood).					
2	Poor presentation of work/self. May look untidy and work may be untidy.					
	Total criteria met					

Scoring: If items 1 or 2 are ticked, then look at the whole of this book and Book 5. If item O is present, then look at Book 4 and complete PIC 2 (in Book 2 or 4). If the answer is yes to either question 1 and 2 plus two or more of the questions marked with an * are ticked then read the sections on handwriting in this book. *If your student profile matches the information within the relevant parts of this library it this does not automatically mean that the student has Graphomotor Dyspraxia. However, this may be a possibility, and a referral to a paediatric occupational therapist (via your GP) or to an education specialist with an interest in handwriting is advised.*

© Jan Poustie 2002. *Identification Solutions for Coordination Difficulties* by Jan Poustie   ISBN 1 901544 87 7

General Index

Resource Index